People That Changed the Course of History

The Story of John Quincy Adams 250 Years After His Birth

Edward Cody Huddleston

Library of Congress Cataloging-in-Publication Data

Names: Huddleston, Edward Cody, 1993- author.
Title: People that changed the course of history : the story of John Quincy
  Adams 250 years after his birth / by Edward Cody Huddleston ; foreword by
  Mike Purdy.
Other titles: Story of John Quincy Adams 250 years after his birth
Description: Ocala, Florida : Atlantic Publishing Group, Inc., 2016. |
  Includes bibliographical references and index. | Audience: Grade 9 to 12.
Identifiers: LCCN 2016043566| ISBN 9781620231456 (alk. paper) | ISBN
  162023145X (alk. paper) | ISBN 9781620232262 (library binding)
Subjects: LCSH: Adams, John Quincy, 1767-1848. | Presidents--United
  States--Biography.
Classification: LCC E377 .H86 2016 | DDC 973.5/5092 [B] --dc23 LC record available at https://lccn.
loc.gov/2016043566

PROJECT MANAGER: Rebekah Sack • rsack@atlantic-pub.com
ASSISTANT EDITOR: Yvonne Bertovich • yvonne.bertovich34@gmail.com
INTERIOR LAYOUT: Steven W. Booth • steven@geniusbookcompany.com
COVER DESIGN: Jackie Miller • millerjackiej@gmail.com
JACKET DESIGN: Steven W. Booth • steven@geniusbookcompany.com

Printed on Recycled Paper

Printed in the United States

Reduce. Reuse.
RECYCLE.

A decade ago, Atlantic Publishing signed the Green Press Initiative. These guidelines promote environmentally friendly practices, such as using recycled stock and vegetable-based inks, avoiding waste, choosing energy-efficient resources, and promoting a no-pulping policy. We now use 100-percent recycled stock on all our books. The results: in one year, switching to post-consumer recycled stock saved 24 mature trees, 5,000 gallons of water, the equivalent of the total energy used for one home in a year, and the equivalent of the greenhouse gases from one car driven for a year.

Over the years, we have adopted a number of dogs from rescues and shelters. First there was Bear and after he passed, Ginger and Scout. Now, we have Kira, another rescue. They have brought immense joy and love not just into our lives, but into the lives of all who met them.

We want you to know a portion of the profits of this book will be donated in Bear, Ginger and Scout's memory to local animal shelters, parks, conservation organizations, and other individuals and nonprofit organizations in need of assistance.

— Douglas & Sherri Brown,
President & Vice-President of Atlantic Publishing

Table of Contents

Foreword

I felt like I'd travelled back in time. As a young congressional intern, I was standing on the floor of the old House of Representatives chamber in the United States Capitol. As my eyes took in the imposing grandeur of the two-story, semicircular room with colossal Corinthian columns around the perimeter, I was reminded of the rich history of the place where the House met for close to four decades. It was here in 1825 that the House selected John Quincy Adams as president over Andrew Jackson after neither won a majority in the Electoral College, and it was in this very room that five presidents were inaugurated.

Beneath my feet was a plaque on the marble floor marking the spot where the desk of Congressman John Quincy Adams once stood. While 18 of our presidents served in the House of Representatives before becoming president, Adams was the only president to serve in the House of Representatives *after* his presidency.

But what really piqued my interest and made me feel like a time traveler was the acoustics of the ornate room. I asked my girlfriend to stand in a marked spot on the opposite side of the room. There, she softly whispered (what exactly I don't remember!) while I stood where Adams used to sit. I could hear her loudly and clearly as though she was right next to me. It was (and still is today) an amazing acoustical quirk!

The long-standing rumor is that John Quincy Adams would sit at his desk pretending to be asleep, when he was really eavesdropping on his opponents in Congress discussing strategy on the other side of the room. I've since learned that the story — as captivating and interesting as it is — isn't true. Adams probably really *was* sleeping at his desk. He was an old man and tired easily. And the acoustics of the room were different when Adams served there with carpeting, desks, and drapes, while annoying echoes reverberated throughout the chamber.

But I felt like I had travelled back in time to where "Old Man Eloquent" had sat for 17 years as a congressman from Massachusetts, where he had stood to argue in his shrill voice against slavery, and where he had slumped over with a fatal stroke after rising to speak.

It's too bad we can't really travel back in time. But by reading about the past, we can come close. We can understand what it was like to live hundreds of years ago. We can gain a fresh appreciation of the people and events of the past. How they have shaped our history as a nation? How does the past impact our lives today? What were the people, like John Quincy Adams, really like?

We might think John Quincy Adams had an easy life, that he always knew what his purpose was, and that he had a clear sense of calling. On the surface, it can certainly look that way when we flip back through the pages of history. With our hindsight, we see how much he accomplished in his lifetime and how it all fit together. He had a famous father, John Adams, who was our second president. As a young boy, John Quincy heard the canon sounds and saw the smoke rising from Revolutionary War battlefields. When he was just 13 years old, he found himself serving as a French translator to the United States ambassador to Russia, the first of many diplomatic posts he held. He was a United States Senator from Massachusetts, Secretary of State, 6th President of the United States, and then a Congressman.

John Quincy Adams was an important bridge between the Revolutionary War era and the debates about slavery leading up to the Civil War. Incredibly, he was personally acquainted with each of our nation's first 17 presidents, from George Washington through Andrew Johnson (with the possible exception of Zachary Taylor, the 12th president), spanning some 80 years of presidential terms.

History can wrap up his life with a neat bow like this. But that is not a complete picture. The life and career of John Quincy Adams took many detours, just as ours do. Sometimes, we don't feel like we are on a clear path. As we try to figure out our place in the world, it's often hard to navigate through the fog of our journey. It's hard to understand how what we're doing is important.

History transports us into another time. When we read about John Quincy Adams, we meet him as a real person with doubts, fears, limitations, hopes, and a somewhat quirky personality, and not just as a distant famous person. As he went through life, he didn't know how things would turn out any more than we know how things will turn out for us.

Adams was rejected for admission to Harvard University the first time he applied. It was embarrassing to him and a blow to his ego and self-confidence. Who among us has not failed, been rejected, and been embarrassed?

After graduating from college, Adams began to study law in order to become an attorney. There was only one problem: He found he hated studying law. The 20-year-old was perplexed by what to do in life. He poured out his anguished heart to his diary:

> "The question, what am I to do in this world recurs to me very frequently; and never without causing great anxiety, and a depression of spirits. My prospects appear darker to me every day, and I am obliged sometimes to drive the subject from my mind and to assume some more agreeable train of thought."

Who among us does not struggle with finding a good career match for our skills and personality? Who among us has not experienced seasons of depression?

As a 23-year-old, John Quincy fell deeply in love with 16-year-old Mary Frazier. "All my hopes of future happiness in this life center on that girl," he wrote to a friend. But Adams' mother, Abigail, embarrassingly intervened and forced him to end the blooming and promising mutual romance. From the heights of hope, his broken heart sank. He was consumed with grief, anguish, and distress. He was crushed. Who among us has not felt the piercing pangs of a broken heart?

In 1828, he was rejected by the voters for a second term as president. Miffed and embarrassed by his defeat, the humorless Adams broke with protocol and slipped out of Washington the night before the inauguration of his successor, Andrew Jackson. It was an occasion that Adams wanted to avoid. He also wasn't overly fond of Jackson, at various times calling him "incompetent," "a barbarian," and "a murderer, an adulterer." But who among us has not experienced the sharp elbows of rejection, and gone to extremes to avoid interactions with people we don't like?

Some people didn't like John Quincy Adams. While he had a first class mind, was task oriented, and was a serious hard worker, he often came across as cold and lacking strong interpersonal skills. He actually knew this about himself, once calling himself "an unsocial savage." Others echoed that sentiment about him. William Henry Harrison, who would go on to be our 9th president, once described Adams as "a disgusting man to do business. Coarse, dirty, and clownish in his address and dress and stiff and abstracted in his opinions, which are drawn from books exclusively." For his part, Adams didn't think too highly of Harrison either saying that he had an "active but shallow mind." And with his sharp tongue, Adams once accused Thomas Jefferson of being "double-dealing, treacherous."

But John Quincy Adams persevered throughout his life. When he was defeated for re-election as president, he didn't just give up. He re-invented himself. He ran for Congress, won, and was re-elected for eight additional terms. Speaking of his election to the House of Representatives, he said, "my election as President of the United States was not half so gratifying."

Like most of us, he forged his own way through life's journey, never really knowing what lay ahead. He grabbed at the second chances that life always gives us, he witnessed a lot of history, and he *made* a lot of history over the course of a public service career spanning over 65 years. Most of us won't become famous and end up in history books like John Quincy Adams, but we do make history each day by the choices we make. History is not just about important people. It's about all of us. It's about how we treat the people in our lives. It's about the decisions we make that help shape our world.

As you read about the remarkable life of John Quincy Adams, put yourself in his shoes. Acknowledge his struggles. Appreciate his successes. See how he persevered. Live with him in his doubts and insecurities. Experience the uncertainty of his unfolding story. Remember that what we know today as his story was for him just an uncertain future. It's the same with us. We don't know how things will turn out in our lives. And so each day, we write new chapters of history. May we take fresh inspiration from the life of John Quincy Adams. Enjoy your travels back in time!

—Mike Purdy

Mike Purdy is a presidential historian and is the founder of PresidentialHistory.com. The website also includes a blog, originally-produced videos that help make presidential history come alive, and other resources. He is a frequent speaker and is often quoted by the media including CNN, *The Wall Street Journal, USA Today,* and Reuters. He graduated from the University of Puget Sound with both undergraduate and graduate degrees in business administration, and also has a Master of Divinity degree from Fuller Theological Seminary.

Introduction: The Storm Before the Calm

The seas grew rough. Then they grew rougher. Everything began to shake, as if the ship itself was trembling with fear.

It had reason to. The *Boston,* an American frigate bound for France, was being pursued by three British warships. Onboard the *Boston* were John Adams and his oldest son. 10-year-old John Quincy Adams put on a brave face for his father, but he understood the danger they were in.

If captured by the British, John Adams would be killed, and John Quincy would be drafted into the Royal Navy.

A thunderous explosion sounded. *This is it,* John Quincy thought. *They've finally hit us.*

Father and son waited in their tiny cabin. They waited for a second explosion. None came. They waited for the *Boston* to sink. It didn't.

No cannonball had struck their ship. Lightning had. That thunderous explosion had come from actual thunder. One sailor was dead and three were injured, but the *Boston* was safe.

At least, it was safe from the British. The storm that set in was massive. Fierce waves and fierce winds tossed the ship around like a toy, threatening to capsize it.

At that moment, reaching Paris alive seemed like a hopeless dream, a dream that would soon sink to the bottom of the Atlantic with the *Boston* and everyone on board.

As they sailed into the storm, John Quincy took a deep breath. He hoped it wouldn't be his last.

Part 1: Seeds of Greatness

Every story starts somewhere. The story of John Quincy Adams started in Braintree, Massachusetts. His early childhood was like the head of a comet. What followed it was longer but not as bright. After witnessing the Battle of Bunker Hill, John Quincy left Braintree with his father on a diplomatic voyage to France. The voyage was terrifying, but they survived. Once in Paris, John Quincy began to familiarize himself with the languages, cultures, and people of Europe. He studied hard and learned fast. He cultivated his mind into fertile soil, and the seeds of greatness took root.

Chapter 1: Braintree Roots

First Breath

On July 11, 1767, John Quincy Adams was born in Braintree, Massachusetts to John and Abigail Adams. He was born at a unique time and in a unique place. Braintree was just six miles south of Boston, the city at the heart of the American Revolution. England ruled the American colonies back then, and most of the colonists hated that. They wanted freedom. Some of them would kill for it, and some of them would die for it. When John Quincy Adams was born, the air was thick with the bloody stench of revolution. With his first breath, he inhaled it.

His parents were brilliant. John Adams was a lawyer who'd studied at Harvard. He'd go on to serve as his nation's first vice president and second president. Abigail Adams, as a woman living in the 1700s, wasn't allowed to go to Harvard. Or anywhere like Harvard. Back then, women weren't given the same opportunities that men were. But that didn't stop her. She became a reader. She read everything she got her hands on until her mind was as sharp and strong as even her husband's.

The birthplace of President John Adams in Quincy, MA.[1]

Life as an Adams

Life in the 1700s wasn't easy. There was a lot less technology and a lot more disease. It was common for a child to die before his first birthday. There was no email, and regular mail could take months to be delivered. When you had a question, you couldn't just do an online search for the answer. You had to try to find it in a book. And not everyone had books. Public libraries were few and far between.

 **Fast Fact:** Speaking of "far," the word meant something different back then. Today, you can fly from Boston to Paris in about seven hours. Back then, traveling that far took about two months by ship. And it was dangerous.

That's the world John Quincy was born into. And he was born into it as an Adams. Life as John and Abigail Adams' first son was stressful. They expected greatness from him — greatness that could only come from incredibly hard work. But John Quincy never collapsed under the pressure. For his entire life, he thrived on it.

He had an older sister. She was named Abigail after her mother. To avoid confusion, she was nicknamed Nabby. (John and Abigail would later have four more children: Susana, Charles, Thomas, and Elizabeth. Sadly, Elizabeth was stillborn, and Susana died as a baby).

The interior of "Peacefield," the home of John and Abigail Adams.[2]

Off to Boston

When John Quincy was nine months old, his father moved the family to Boston, bringing them straight into the heart of the American Revolution. He thought that moving to Boston would give him the chance to make a name for himself as a lawyer.

He thought right.

The Spark That Set the World on Fire

Two years after moving to Boston, John Adam's decision to leave his 95-acre farm in Braintree paid off. He was given his most important case ever.

Up until that point, the fight for American independence hadn't really been a fight. Both sides fought with words, but there hadn't been much violence. That changed on March 5, 1770. Five Americans were killed and six were injured by British gunfire.

The event, which became known as the Boston Massacre, began when an American named Edward Garrick taunted British officer John Goldfinch. Garrick, a wigmaker's apprentice, taunted Goldfinch for owing money to Garrick's master. Goldfinch, it turns out, had already paid the bill. He ignored the insults, but Hugh White, a British soldier, overheard what was happening. He told the American to show respect to Goldfinch. Garrick refused. One insult led to another. Then, White hit Garrick in the head with his musket. This angered onlookers who formed an angry mob.

The mob was led by an escaped slave named Crispus Attucks. Attucks threw snowballs at the British soldiers (there were eight soldiers at this point) and dared them to shoot him. Not in the mood for a snowball fight, a soldier complied. Attucks became the first person to die in the Revolutionary War. More soldiers opened fire, and two more Americans, Samuel Gray and James

Caldwell, quickly died alongside Attucks. Of the six who were injured, Samuel Maverick and Patrick Carr later died of their injuries.

The soldiers involved in the incident were arrested and put on trial. In charge of their defense was John Adams. He was chosen by British Governor Thomas Hutchinson because of his anti-British views, so the colonists couldn't accuse the soldiers of getting special treatment. Adams argued to an American jury that the soldiers' lives were in danger, and they were acting in self-defense. The jury agreed. Mostly.

Six of the eight soldiers were found innocent. However, Matthew Killroy and Hugh Montgomery were convicted of manslaughter.

Fast Fact: Killroy and Montgomery had the letter "M" (for murder) branded on their right thumbs.

Even though most of the soldiers were found innocent, the political damage had already been done. Americans hated British rule more than ever before. John Adams himself later wrote that during the Boston Massacre, "the foundation of American independence was laid."

His victory in court catapulted John Adams to fame, and he used that fame to win election to Massachusetts' House of Representatives.

The Battle of Bunker Hill

Five years passed. During those years, conflict between American rebels and British loyalists escalated. Boston became a war zone, and John Adams moved his family back to Braintree for safety.

John Adams then left Braintree to go to Philadelphia. There, delegates met to discuss how the American colonies could free themselves from British rule. It was the second time delegates had a meeting like this, and it was called the Second Continental Congress. (John Adams had also attended the First Continental Congress, where representatives agreed to boycott imports of British goods.) Members of the Second Continental Congress included four other future American presidents:

1. George Washington
2. Thomas Jefferson
3. James Madison
4. James Monroe

Back in Braintree, the sound of cannon fire rumbled through the city. Abigail knew what that meant. The war was closer to home than ever. American and British soldiers were fighting just to the north. She got her four kids — Nabby, John Quincy, Charles, and Thomas — and took them with her to the top of Penn's hill. And there, just a short walk from their house, they watched the battle unfold.

British forces wanted to capture the hills of Charlestown (a neighborhood in Boston) to use to rain cannonballs down on the rest of the city. Over 3,000 British troops went into battle. They wore red uniforms and marched in straight lines. American soldiers, who numbered about 2,400, gunned down row after row of redcoats. But, after 12 hours of soul-crushing battle, most of the Americans ran out of ammunition, and the British overwhelmed them.

Lithograph of The Battle of Bunker Hill by Nathanial Currier after a painting by J. Trumbull from June 17, 1775.[3]

The Americans retreated, and British forces captured Charlestown. When the dust had settled and the smoke had cleared, over 1,000 British troops lay dead or wounded. The American casualties were less than half of that. Among the dead was Joseph Warren, the Adams family's doctor and close friend.

John Quincy watched the smoke rise from Charlestown as it burned. Witnessing the battle, even from a distance, affected him greatly. "I saw with my own eyes the fires of Charlestown… and witnessed the tears of my mother and mingled them with my own at the fall of Dr. Joseph Warren, a dear friend of my father and a beloved physician to me" (Frank).

His Father's Shadow

Life without his father took a psychological toll on John Quincy, but it didn't stop him. He studied hard and learned fast.

John Adams knew his son had potential. He wrote to Abigail, "I am under no apprehension about his proficiency in learning. With his capacities and opportunities, he cannot fail to acquire knowledge. But let him know that the sentiments of his heart are more important than the furniture of his head" (Burleigh).

John Adams was, at this point, a distant but godlike figure in his son's eyes. Motivated by his father's fame and bravery, John Quincy became determined to succeed. He studied history. He mastered Greek and Latin. He read Shakespeare, Milton, and the Bible.

His life was stressful. Focusing on his studies wasn't easy when the threat of British troops marching over Penn's Hill to wreak havoc on Braintree was constantly on his mind. Also on his mind was the fact that the British had identified John Adams as a threat and had called for his arrest and execution.

He later wrote that, "In my early childhood, a deep and inexhaustible abhorrence of war was placed in my bosom in the terror of a war then raged by Britain" (Kaplan).

Any day, a letter could have arrived saying that his father had been shot, hanged, or beheaded. And, every day, he, his mother, and his siblings prayed that such a letter wouldn't come.

Thankfully, for them and for America, it never did. But many letters did come, letters from John Adams asking about his son's progress and offering advice on his studies. John Quincy read them religiously. And he followed them, quite literally, to the letter.

Off to France

In January of 1778, two bombshells were dropped on John Quincy's life. The first: his father had been selected by the Second Continental Congress to go to France. There, he'd join Benjamin Franklin in seeking French aid in the war against England. The second: John Quincy would be going with him.

John Adams hated being away from his oldest son. By bringing John Quincy, he hoped they could repair the damage that distance had caused their relationship. He was right.

Horrifying danger has a way of bringing people together.

Sources

1   Photo Credit: Daniel M. Silva / Shutterstock.com

2   Photo Credit: Joseph Sohm / Shutterstock.com

3   Photo Credit: Everett Historical / Shutterstock.com

Chapter 2: Life in France

A Treacherous Voyage

"Mr. Adams, you're embarking under most threatening signs. The Heavens frown! The clouds roll! The hollow winds howl!" These are the words of a distant cousin of John Adams, who advised him and his son not to leave for Paris, believing their voyage to be doomed.

She seemed crazy then. Six days later, when they were out at sea, three British ships appeared on the horizon. They spotted the American frigate and gave chase. As they closed in on the *Boston,* the witch-like cackling of the old woman echoed in the mind of John Quincy.

The chase lasted hours. Then an entire day. Then another day. That evening, the *Boston* was still out of range of British cannon fire. The chase would have continued, but a new danger presented itself.

That night, John Adams and his son were in bed, trying to rest, when an ear-shattering noise exploded above them. A British cannon, they figured. They huddled together, terrified, as they waited for a second explosion. It didn't come.

A cannonball hadn't struck their ship. Lightning had. It had killed a sailor and injured three more, but the *Boston* was safe. At least, it was safe from the British, who could no longer give chase. A huge storm had overtaken the *Boston*. "To describe the ocean, the waves, the winds … is impossible," John Adams wrote in his journal. "No place or person was dry" (Butterfield).

Fast Fact: Throughout the ordeal, John Quincy showed no sign of fear. He took turns manning the pumps that kept the ship from filling with seawater. Eventually, the storm passed, and John Quincy returned to French, his latest subject of study. He would speak it almost fluently by the time they reached France.

Arriving at Last

April 1, 1778, about six weeks after setting sail, the *Boston* docked at Bordeaux.

The two future presidents, thrilled to be on dry land, took a few days to explore the city. They went to operas. They went to plays. And they sampled the food, finding it delicious.

The new opera in Paris, France, in the 1800s.[1]

Then the Adams duo began their journey to Paris, which took four days. On arrival, they realized that they couldn't afford a decent place to stay. Luckily, Benjamin Franklin greeted them warmly and invited them to live with him in his mansion.

It wasn't like living on a farm in Massachusetts. Paris was the social hub of Europe. Franklin held elegant parties with huge feasts and an endless supply of expensive wine. He had servants to wait on himself and his guests.

But that sort of thing wasn't to John Adams' taste. He was a strict man who lived a disciplined life. Just a week after moving into Franklin's mansion, he sent John Quincy to boarding school.

Always a quick study, he perfected his French and Latin. He also learned to dance, fence, and draw.

Meanwhile, his father was miserable. He disliked the Paris social scene, and it disliked him. After only a month in the city, he wrote to the Second Continental Congress, asking for permission to return home.

Going Home

Ten months later, permission was granted. John Adams spent those months sending reports to Congress about the political situation in France. John Quincy spent them studying. When it was time to go, they departed Paris in a horse-drawn carriage. From there, they headed 240 miles west to Nantes.

It was in Nantes that they were to baoard their ship, the *Alliance.* But it wasn't there. Back in those days of pirating and constant naval combat, it was common for ships to vanish between ports. John Quincy and his father spent almost two months waiting for the *Alliance,* knowing that it might have been resting at the bottom of the sea.

Luckily, it wasn't. On April 22, the *Alliance* finally docked at Nantes. The Adamses were thrilled to be going home. Until they were told they wouldn't be going home.

The *Alliance* wasn't being used for transportation any more. Instead, the French government planned to use it to sink British cargo ships. They placed it under the authority of Revolutionary War hero John Paul Jones.

John Paul Jones lived about a hundred miles away in Lorient. That happened to be where the Adamses traveled next, hoping to find a ship headed for the colonies that they could board. They didn't find one right away, but they did find John Paul Jones himself, and had dinner in his home.

Finally, John Adams secured passage on a ship named *Sensible,* and he and John Quincy set sail for the colonies.

Back in Boston

Their six-week voyage across the Atlantic was peaceful. John Quincy used his time on the *Sensible* to teach two other passengers, both of them French diplomats, to speak English.

They reached Boston in early August and neither expected to ever set foot in Europe again.

John Adams, thanks to the success of his book, *Thoughts on Government,* was called on by his countrymen to write the Massachusetts Constitution.

Fast Fact: The Constitution of the Commonwealth of Massachusetts is the oldest constitution that's still in use anywhere in the world.

It guaranteed rights to all citizens, including freedom of speech, freedom of religion, freedom of press, and freedom to bear arms. It gave any free citizen accused of a crime the right to a trial by jury, and it balanced legal authority between three branches of government.

"We the People" are the opening words of the preamble to the Constitution of the United States of America.[2]

First: **the executive branch**. It was headed by the governor and included several lessor offices and executive departments. This branch of government enforced laws. Second: **the legislative branch**. It consisted of the Massachusetts Senate and House of Representatives. This branch of government wrote laws. The third: **the judicial branch**. It consisted of the Massachusetts Supreme Court and numerous lower-level courts. This branch of government interpreted laws, deciding which of them applied to a given situation.

After John Adams finished writing the Massachusetts Constitution, he received a letter from the Second Continental Congress. He was to return to France, this time as the colonies' sole ambassador. While in France, he'd informed Congress that he believed having more than one ambassador to the nation was unnecessary. Of course, he'd intended for the position to go to Benjamin Franklin, not himself. But, without a word of complaint to Congress, he accepted it.

Returning to France

On November 13, 1779, John Adams and John Quincy boarded the *Sensible* and departed for France again. John Adams also brought his middle son, Charles, his cousin, John Thaxter, and a lawyer, Francis Dana, who would serve as his secretary.

The day before they set sail, John Quincy started a project, one that he would invest time in nearly every day for the rest of his life. He titled it "A Journal by Me JQA VOL 1." The journal, which would record his feelings, thoughts, and what happened in his life for the next 69 years, began with the words:

"1779 November Friday 12th. This morning at about 11 o'clock I took leave of my mama" (Levin).

Strong storms tattered the *Sensible's* sails and threatened to sink the frigate. The thick, black clouds, howling winds, and torrents of rain were overwhelming. Proper navigation was impossible. But, after just under than a month at sea, their luck changed. The crew spotted land!

However, it wasn't France. They'd been thrown off course and were sailing off the coast of Spain. But they didn't care. Land was land. They docked in Ferrol, a small port in northwest Spain.

John Adams and company would have to make the rest of their journey by land. But that wasn't easy either. Heavy rain had turned the roads to mud, which made travel miserable.

Their situation wasn't all bad, though. The path they took into France was known for crime. Highwaymen armed with swords, pistols, and muskets would ambush travelers and steal their luggage. At least, that's what they did on sunny days. Lucky for the travelers, the awful weather kept them at bay.

They didn't feel lucky, though. They contracted severe colds, which added to their misery.

Finally, after a punishing journey, they reached the city of Bilbao on January 15, 1780. At long last, they could rest. The difficult part of their journey was over. After relaxing for a few days, they departed for France and arrived in Paris on February 9.

John Quincy and Charles were enrolled in a boarding school. They practiced writing in Greek, Latin, French, and English. They also studied arithmetic and fractions and learned to draw.

Harvest of Knowledge

John Adams assumed his role as diplomat, but found the French uninterested in providing further military aid to the United States.

This, it turns out, was due to the fact that the French wanted to give the United States just enough strength to resist England. Their idea was that weakening both sides would allow them to invade British-owned territories in Canada.

John Adams realized this, so he took his sons and cousin with him and departed for the Netherlands on July 27, 1780. He knew that getting Holland to recognize the United States as a nation would improve its standing around the world.

They arrived in Amsterdam without incident, and John Adams enrolled his sons in the Latin academy. However, neither boy spoke Dutch well enough to keep up with the other students, so John Adams soon withdrew them.

John Thaxter was taking classes at the University of Leiden. He began bringing the boys with him to class and tutoring them. The boys learned fast, and after only a few months of study, 13-year-old John Quincy was admitted to the university as a full-time student. A few months later, his brother was also admitted.

This is a Dutch painting of Amsterdam in the early 1800s by Eduard Alexander Hilverdink.[3]

John and Abigail were overcome with pride. "What a harvest of true knowledge you may gather," Abigail wrote to John Quincy, "from the numberless and varied scenes through which you pass..." (Levin).

John Quincy's brilliance didn't go unrecognized by the locals, either. Lawyer and journalist Jean Luzac met the boy and was astonished by his level of intelligence; he soon befriended him. John Quincy introduced Luzac to his father. Their meeting lead to Luzac supporting Dutch aid to the United States and recognition of it as an independent nation.

It was the first time John Quincy changed history.

It wouldn't be the last.

Sources

1   Photo Credit: Morphart Creation / Shutterstock.com
2   Photo Credit: David Smart / Shutterstock.com
3   Photo Credit: Everett – Art / Shutterstock.com

Chapter 3: To Russia

John Quincy's First Job

Jean Luzac wasn't the only one impressed with John Quincy. Francis Dana recognized the boy's genius, and when Dana was appointed by Congress to serve as foreign minister to Russia, he decided to bring John Quincy along.

In those days, French was spoken by most of the European upper-class. And, as Francis Dana spoke neither Russian nor French, he needed a translator. Bringing a thirteen-year-old to serve as a translator wasn't exactly normal, but neither was John Quincy.

On July 7, 1781, the two set off for Saint Petersburg, which was then the capital of Russia. Their journey, which lasted about 2,000 miles, took them through Berlin. It was there that John Quincy encountered slavery for the first time.

"*They are bought and sold like so many beasts, and are sometimes even changed for dogs and horses. Their masters have even the right of life and death over them, and if they kill one of them they are only obliged to pay a trifling fine*" (Butterfield).

Boredom

Finally, the deep freeze thawed, and life was easier, but not more productive. Francis Dana made no political progress in Russia, though he and John Quincy remained there for over a year.

John Quincy spent that year doing what he always did when he had free time: reading. He became increasingly interested in Cicero, the Greek orator and philosopher. He first encountered Cicero years earlier, but, as he grew, so did his love for the man who'd once said:

"*A room without books is like a body without a soul*" (Braude).

John Quincy also took the time to write to his father who, though impressed with his son's reading list, was annoyed by his poor penmanship. "I don't perceive that you take pains enough with your handwriting... if you now in your youth resolutely conquer your impatience, and resolve never to write the most familiar letter or trifling card without attention and care, it will save you a vast deal of time, and trouble too, every day of your whole life" (Butterfield).

That annoyed John Quincy, who didn't reply for more than a month. When he did, he wrote in French, a language he understood better than his father, who complained that his son was more skillful in French than in his native tongue.

John Quincy also exchanged letters with his mother, who stressed to him the importance of dressing and behaving well. John Quincy often neglected to reply to these letters, and was probably annoyed by them.

But, despite the nagging, John Quincy missed his parents, and, when his father suggested he leave Russia and join him in the Netherlands, he agreed.

Off On His Own

On October 30, 1782, Jon Quincy left Saint Petersburg. After a journey (by boat and carriage) that took him through Finland and across the Baltic Sea, he was in Sweden. Instead of continuing his journey right away, he found the beautiful country, and its beautiful women, too charming to leave. Later, he even referred to Sweden as the "land of lovely dames."

What was John Quincy Adams really like?
John Quincy, happy to be free from the boredom of
life in Saint Petersburg, spent his time dancing, playing
cards, and flirting with young women. The bookworm
showed another side to his personality. He even started
staying out late and returning to his room after sunrise.

While John Quincy was busy being a teenager, his parents were
busy being parents. They worried about their son. Abigail was
especially concerned. She wrote to her husband, "He has been
less under your Eye than I could wish, but never I dare say without your advise and instruction. If he does not return this winter, I wish you to remind him, that he has forgotten to use his
pen, to his Friends upon this Side the water" (Butterfield).

On February 11, 1783, after more than two months of explor-
ing Sweden, John Quincy's journey to the Netherlands resumed.
He traveled through Denmark and Germany, taking plenty of
time to stop and socialize in both countries.

John Quincy arrived in The Hague on April 21, but, because his
father had departed for Paris, their reunion was delayed. John
Adams had been called upon to aid in negotiating a peace treaty
with the British.

It wasn't until July 22 that John Adams finally got to see his son
again. He was shocked.

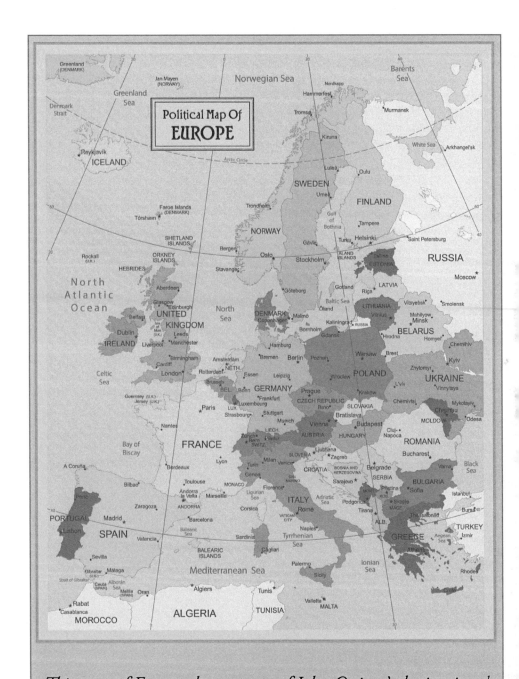

This map of Europe shows many of John Quincy's destinations.[1]

Sources

1   Photo Credit: ekler / Shutterstock.com

Chapter 4: A Boy Becomes a Man

Father and Son

For the first time in his life, John Adams looked up at his son. The 15-year-old was now slightly taller than his father, and his growth was more than physical. He walked, talked, and carried himself like an adult.

John Adams was overjoyed. He wrote to Abigail, "John is a great comfort to me. He is everything you could wish him. Wholly devoted to his studies, he has made a progress which gives me entire satisfaction" (Butterfield).

John Quincy, who had spent three months waiting in The Hague with his nose buried in books, joined his father when he returned to Paris to continue talks with the British.

In Paris, John Quincy acted as secretary for the American diplomats. The sixteen-year-old helped his father and Benjamin

Franklin edit important legal documents. He enjoyed the work and was proud to be trusted with it.

Negotiations went well, and the Treaty of Paris was signed on September 3, 1783, ending the Revolutionary War. It acknowledged the United States of America as its own nation, free from British rule. It also established boundaries between the United States and Britain's remaining territory in North America.

With the treaty signed, the Adamses planned to return to Braintree. They put that plan on hold when John Adams became sick. What his illness was isn't known, but it may have been caused by stress. He spent more than a month trying to recover. Deciding that they needed a vacation, he and John Quincy left France to visit England.

While his father rested, John Quincy spent the next few months soaking in English life and culture. He went on trips to art galleries, libraries, and theaters, but John Adams still felt sick.

They needed to return to the Netherlands. The United States had ordered John Adams to secure new loans from the Dutch government. The problem was traveling there. John Adams thought that the voyage might kill him.

On January 2, 1784, he and John Quincy began their journey anyway. The voyage across the North Sea took 10 days, but they survived. They arrived in The Hague and resumed their lives. John Quincy returned to his studies, and John Adams pursued the loans, his health having suddenly improved.

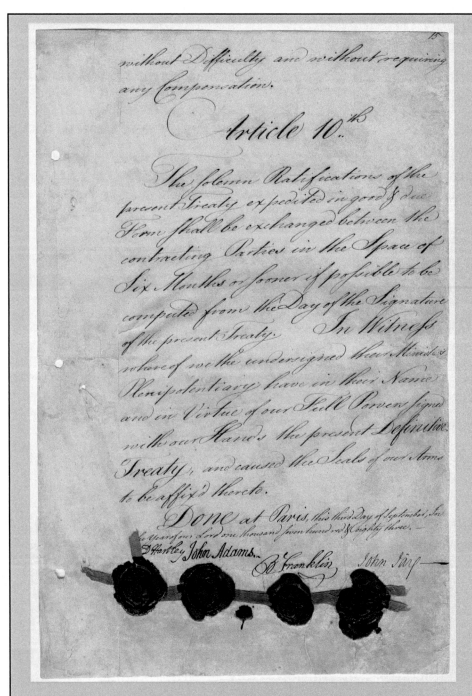

The second page of the Treaty of Paris in 1783 shows the signatures of John Adams, Benjamin Franklin, and John Jay.[1]

A Family Reunion

John Quincy left the Netherlands in May of 1784 to meet his mother and sister. Abigail and Nabby had grown sick of waiting for the Adams men to return to Boston and boarded a ship bound for Britain. There they would meet John Quincy, and the three would travel to Paris to meet John Adams, who had diplomatic business there.

Abigail and Nabby hadn't seen John Quincy in four years, and the sight of him almost startled them speechless. "Nothing but the Eyes at first sight appeared what he once was," Abigail wrote. "His appearance is that of a Man…" (Levin).

After a warm reunion and a brief stay in London, the trio of Adamses left England to meet John Adams in Paris, and the entire family was together at last.

John's Decision

When Abigail Adams came to Europe, she brought her motherly concerns with her. Her son was becoming a man, a man with great potential. She wanted to make sure he didn't waste it.

For as long as John Quincy had been alive, his parents had wanted him to be a leader — a towering political figure like his father. That meant going to Harvard, the oldest and most respected college in America. But, in 1784, the Netherlands' University of Leiden was a rich breeding ground of ideas, a cultural centerpiece in Europe. John Quincy wanted to resume his studies there.

He had spent his teenage years in Europe, and the United States didn't feel like home anymore. John Quincy enjoyed an almost celebrity status in Paris, spending evenings at huge parties and socializing with Thomas Jefferson and Marquis de Lafayette. And he'd noticed the stress that a life in politics had caused his father who, though not yet fifty, looked old and exhausted.

Later that year, John Adams was appointed the United States' first foreign minister to England. It was an important job, and it may have had a role in John Quincy's decision.

After much thought, he decided to go to Harvard, the school that his father and grandfather had both attended. John Adams wasted no time writing a letter to Harvard's president, Joseph Willard. In the letter, he described John Quincy's travels, studies, and near-completion of a degree at the University of Leiden. He insisted that his son be allowed to enter Harvard as a member of either the junior or senior class. A student as advanced as John Quincy shouldn't be admitted as a freshman or sophomore.

Willard refused to let John Quincy into the senior class, the junior class, or even Harvard itself, without testing him first. But, if he tested well, Willard assured John Adams that his son would be given advanced placement. Willard, out of respect for John Adams' service to the United States, agreed not to charge tuition.

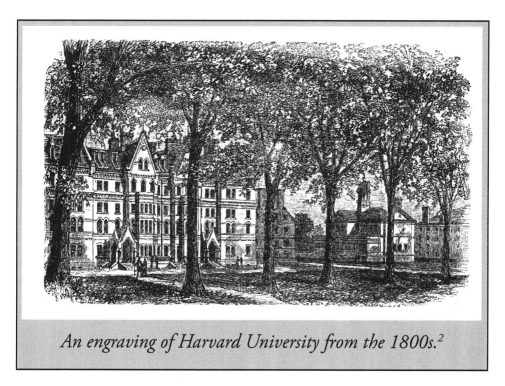

An engraving of Harvard University from the 1800s.[2]

John Adams, not doubting his son for a second, agreed to these terms. The family was short on funds; free tuition was a tempting offer. Besides, John Quincy was a genius.

How hard could one test be?

Sources

1   Photo Credit: Everett Historical / Shutterstock.com
2   Photo Credit: Morphart Creation / Shutterstock.com

Part 2: The Rise to Relevance

John Quincy was staring down adulthood like the barrel of a rifle. In his crosshairs was a promising career as a lawyer and public servant. Not an easy target, but he was ready to take his best shot.

At least, he hoped he was. The man who would go on to be present for some of the most important events in early American history, and not just as an observer, was plagued by self-doubt. The threat of failure haunted his thoughts.

John Quincy didn't know if he could face the world. And he certainly didn't know if he could change it.

Chapter 5: Harvard

The Willard Problem

John Quincy left his family and friends on May 12, 1785. He arrived in New York on July 18, and after taking time to socialize with local political figures (New York was the nation's capital city at the time), he set off for Boston. From there, he went to Braintree where his aunt Mary Cranch and her family greeted him warmly.

Mary Cranch was impressed by her nephew, and she wrote to Abigail, "I have already discovered a strength of mind, a memory, a soundness of judgment which I have seldom seen united in one so young."

Joseph Willard disagreed. On August 21, John Quincy traveled to Cambridge and met with Harvard's president. Willard was a strict, bitter, old-fashioned man. He was a reverend and a mathematician who cared little for Europe and its culture. He cared even less for the upbeat, friendly teenager who, though only sixteen years old, had likely already achieved more in life than Willard himself.

Willard tested John Quincy in Latin and Greek. He then told the boy that he'd failed, and he should apply next year. John Quincy was shocked. He'd taken it for granted that he'd pass.

He moved to Haverhill, a town about 35 miles from Cambridge. There, he lived with his uncle, John Shaw. Shaw, a reverend and tutor, helped John Quincy prepare to reapply to Harvard.

If his life had been a movie, the following months would have been a montage. And, in every scene, he would have had a book in his hands. Plato's dialogues, Cicero's orations, Homer's epics, *The Iliad* and *The Odyssey*, and Virgil's *Aeneid* were all consumed by his ravenous mind. His reading list also included works by English philosopher John Locke.

John Quincy, after almost seven months of study, returned to Harvard on March 14, 1786. This time, he wasn't tested by Willard alone. Eight other members of the Harvard faculty were present to ensure fairness.

He was tested in Greek. He was tested in Latin. He was tested in logic, geography, and mathematics. Finally, after witnessing John Quincy run a mental marathon, Willard finally said it.

"You're admitted, Adams" (Nagel).

College Life

John Quincy was admitted as a junior. He moved into his room on campus and began his studies.

But there wasn't much to study. John Quincy found that the Harvard faculty, for all of their smug arrogance, had little to teach him that he hadn't already learned.

Life on campus was chaotic. The students were often drunk. On one night, John Quincy noted in his diary that a group of them got more drunk than usual and began shattering windows around the campus.

What was John Quincy really like as a college student? John Quincy never took to vandalism, but he did enjoy himself. He stayed out late, sometimes dancing until after 4 a.m. He skipped classes to go for walks and socialize with other students. He read, wrote, and even took up playing the flute. Despite the rocky start, life as a Harvard student was a joyful time in his life.

And then it was over. Fifteen months after being admitted to Harvard, John Quincy had earned his degree, placing second in his class of 51 students.

Graduation

Oration (the art of speaking well) fascinated John Quincy. So, on April 18, 1787, he gave a speech at his graduation ceremony. It addressed the need for a stronger central government for the United States. At that time, the United States was so much a country as it was 13 separate countries working together. And they weren't working together well.

Politicians in each state went to the capital with only the interests of their own people in mind, and no concern for what was best for the country as a whole. John Quincy saw this for the problem it was, and gave a passionate speech about it.

His speech was well-received, even by Willard. In a letter to John Adams, he wrote that John Quincy "...bids fair to become a distinguished character" (Nagel).

Having put Harvard behind him, John Quincy prepared to move on to the next chapter in his life. He planned to follow in his father's footsteps and become a lawyer. By this point, he'd walked many miles in his father's shoes. He was named after him. He'd gone to the same college as him. His attempts to carve out an identity for himself had been stamped out by his mother. For as long as he could remember, she'd pleaded with, begged and urged him to be like John Adams.

And he would be like his father in terms of being a great person who would achieve great things. But his road to greatness wasn't what anyone, certainly not Abigail Adams, could have predicted.

After graduating from Harvard, John Quincy packed up his things and set off for Newburyport. There, he would begin studying to be a lawyer, a career choice he would soon grow to hate.

Chapter 6: Life as a Legal Scholar

Dealing with Depression

John Quincy arrived in Newburyport on September 7 to begin his legal studies under Theophilus Parsons, a respected attorney.

Four of John Quincy's classmates from Harvard were also studying under Parsons. Their friendship was enough to keep him from feeling lonely, but not enough to keep him from feeling miserable.

He discovered that he hated being a lawyer and nearly gave it up. In fact, he probably would have, but the fact that he still depended on his parents for money disgusted him. He believed that, as a lawyer, he'd make a good living and free himself from the feeling of being a burden.

So he studied, reading dense, dry legal books for hours a day. If it were really possible to die of boredom, he would have passed away with a law book clutched in his hands. In fact, he mentioned wanting to die in his journal, writing "take me from this earth before I curse the day of my birth!" (Adams).

But then something happened that he could never have expected — something that would change his life forever.

Young Love

John Quincy wasn't much of a ladies' man. He often made note of attractive women in his journal, and casual flirting was easy for him, but the 22-year-old had never been in a relationship. Back then, the world of dating was a lot different. Men weren't considered suitable partners until they'd become actual men. That meant having a job and a steady income. John Quincy, for all of his genius and all of his hard work, had neither.

The process of getting to know a person you liked was called courting, and it was formal by today's standards. What your sweetheart's parents thought about you was hugely important, as was your own family's social standing. Getting to know your future husband or wife wasn't easy, because, chances are, you wouldn't be given much time alone.

For the first two decades of his life, John Quincy had shown little interest in finding a partner. That changed when he met Mary Frazier. The soft-spoken, blonde 15-year-old was gorgeous, kindhearted, and intelligent. John Quincy found her so attractive that he wrote poetry about her:

> *Kind nature formed of purest white her skin,*
> *An emblem of her innocence within;*
> *And called on cheerful Health, her aid to lend,*
> *The roses' colors in her cheeks to blend,*
> *While Venus added, to complete the fair,*
> *The eyes blue languish and the golden hair.*
> *But fair superior charms exalt her mind,*
> *Adorned by nature and by art refined.*

The young couple spent an increasing amount of time together at the Frazier home. They went on walks, discussed their plans for the future, and, before long, they fell in love.

But sadly, their romance was doomed from the start. Mary, sticking with the customs of the time, insisted that John Quincy give her a formal and public marriage proposal. Since he lacked the income to support a bride, he refused.

And with that, the two separated, both of them heartbroken. Mary Frazier would go on to die of an illness when she was only 30 years old. John Quincy, even as an old man, would never forget her.

 **Fast Fact:** Decades after Mary passed away, an elderly John Quincy was mailed a hand-written copy of his love poem inspired by her. He recognized the handwriting. She'd made the copy herself and kept it with her until she died.

A deeply saddened John Quincy continued his legal studies. The future president wrote in his journal, "My prospects appear darker to me every day."

His prospects didn't just appear dark because he was single again. They appeared dark because his father's shined so brightly. January 7, 1789, John Adams was appointed by Congress to serve as the United States' first vice president. It was a huge honor, one John Quincy thought he'd never equal.

Chapter 7:
A Career
Change

Legal Woes

In the summer of 1790, John Quincy passed the Massachusetts bar exam. He was ready to start his career as a lawyer.

Or so he thought. He moved to Boston, set up shop in a building owned by his father, and opened for business. But little business came. As the vice president's son, he'd expected the gravity of his name to draw in clients. When that failed to happen, his despair deepened. Not only had he picked a career he didn't like, but he was failing at it.

After receiving letters from their son about his depressed state, John and Abigail Adams became concerned for his mental health. They urged him to take a break and join them in Philadelphia, which was recently assigned the role of being the United States' capital city. When John Quincy got there, he met congressmen, senators, and judges — the people who ran the country. He knew he belonged among them.

After spending several weeks with his parents, he returned to Boston and resumed work. Business was as slow as before, so he had plenty of free time. He used it to write.

An Important Essay

Thomas Paine and Thomas Jefferson were icons of the American Revolution, and both were known for their political writings. John Quincy respected both of them. (In fact, he was close friends with Thomas Jefferson.) Thomas Paine had recently published a book, *The Rights of Man.*

The 90,000-word book called for the people of England to overthrow their king, destroy their government, and replace it with a direct democracy. He argued that the French Revolution, in which the French citizens had overthrown their king, had set an example that the English should follow. Thomas Jefferson had endorsed the book. John Quincy, however, despised it. He wrote that "[Paine] supposes the essence of a free government to be the submission of the minority to the will of the majority… in a free government the minority never can be under an obligation to sacrifice their rights to the will of the majority."

John Quincy's first letter (ten more would soon follow) was first published in the *Columbian Centinel,* a Boston newspaper. It couldn't have come at a better time.

The French Revolution, which had begun in 1789 and wouldn't end until 1799, was turning bloody. People were being shot, stabbed, beheaded, and burned alive — often for little or no reason.

Publicola, which John Quincy named his series of letters, was published throughout the United States. It then went on to be published in London, Scotland, and Ireland. Readers across two continents identified with its message. From the seclusion of his writing desk, John Quincy had affected the political landscape of the world.

The Political Stage

After the success of *Publicola,* John Quincy began to involve himself in local politics. He tried and failed to reform Boston's police system. He then drafted a law that declared the northern region of Braintree to be a separate city, which he named Quincy.

He seemed content with his life at this point. Business had picked up, and his writings gave him a creative outlet and political voice. It seemed as though John Quincy had found his place in the world.

George Washington had other ideas. He'd read John Quincy's essay, and was impressed by the young man's intellect. (He was also thrilled to have his support, as the essay condemned the pro-French movement in the United States, which was pushing

Washington to declare another war on England.) He appointed John Quincy to serve as American minister to the Netherlands. It was, John Adams wrote in a letter to his son, a job that would "require all your prudence and all your other virtues as well as all your talents."

At first, he didn't want the job. He believed that he'd only been given it because of his father's influence. That may have been true, but when the motion to send him to the Netherlands was approved by the Senate without a single member voting against it, John Quincy changed his mind.

Chapter 8: The Diplomat

Minister to the Netherlands

On August 19, 1794, John Quincy left Boston to go to the Netherlands. His brother Thomas, who'd agreed to work as John Quincy's secretary, joined him. The voyage went smoothly, except for the seasickness that plagued both of them, and the ship *Alfred* delivered them to England on October 15. From the port of Deal, they traveled to London.

As they neared the city, something happened that terrified John Quincy. A trunk of important documents that he'd been entrusted to deliver was nearly stolen from his carriage. Someone had cut the strap that held it in place and expected it to fall from the carriage unnoticed. Luckily for John Quincy, he heard the *crash* of the trunk hitting the road behind him. Realizing that someone was trying to steal the documents, he kept a careful eye on the trunk for the rest of the journey. The paperwork inside of it had been entrusted to him by George Washington himself. It contained crucial information regarding the USA's policies toward Britain, and losing it would have embarrassed John Quincy and his entire country.

After getting the trunk to its destination and taking time to relax, John Quincy and Thomas resumed their journey. They arrived in The Hague on October 31. Around that time, France declared war on England, Spain, and the Netherlands. A few months after the Adams brothers arrived in The Hague, French troops poured into the city.

This could have meant extreme danger for John Quincy. But it didn't. His command of the French language made it easy for him to get along with the soldiers, who did surprisingly little to disturb life in the city.

In fact, John Quincy's life in the Netherlands turned out to be pretty boring. He spent massive amounts of time writing reports about the political goings-on of Europe. However, that didn't seem to bother him much. He'd gotten out of being a lawyer and was finally earning a decent living.

In his reports to the United States, John Quincy repeated an idea he'd defended in his famous essay: neutrality. As Europe suffered from constant outbreaks of war, the United States could prosper if it stayed neutral and avoided conflict. This opinion of John Quincy's stemmed from a deeper belief: the belief that the United States was its own country, independent from European rule. It seemed simple enough, but foreign nations were eager to drag the U.S. into fighting their battles for them, and they weren't above using threats and bribes to get what they wanted.

The spring after John Quincy arrived in the Netherlands, the nation's government signed a treaty with France. The treaty legally reduced the Netherlands into little more than a French colony, but left much of its government intact. John Quincy's mission wasn't affected by this, except that it gave him more to report.

On October 20, 1795, John Quincy left the Netherlands. He'd been called away to England to oversee the signing of the Jay Treaty. The Jay Treaty returned some British property confiscated during the Revolutionary War in exchange for the British vacating posts held in the American northwest and allowing American trade in the Indies.

Bad weather delayed his voyage, and by the time he arrived in England, the treaty had been signed. The trip should have been a complete waste. But it wasn't.

While in England, John Quincy met Louisa Johnson. At 20 years of age, she was the second oldest child of American merchant Joshua Johnson's eight children. She was beautiful, intelligent and well-spoken in both French and English. She and John Quincy talked, went for walks, and that's pretty much it. (Courting back then wasn't as fun as modern dating.)

When John Quincy returned to the Netherlands, his heart stayed behind in England, entrusted to Louisa. However, he wasn't ready to propose yet. His position as minister to the Netherlands only earned him $4,500 a year.

An engraving of First Lady Louisa Catherine Adams.[1]

Fast Fact: A salary of $4,500 a year, adjusted for inflation, would be like $82,000 a year today. However, this didn't go nearly as far in Europe as it would have in the United States.

After paying his brother's wages, John Quincy lacked the funds to support a family. Luckily for the young couple, that would change soon.

A Promotion

George Washington was impressed with John Quincy's work in the Netherlands. In fact, he was so impressed that he nominated him to be appointed minister to Portugal. The pay was twice what John Quincy was earning in The Hague, plus he'd have a $4,500 yearly budget for expenses.

However, before the nomination could be confirmed by the Senate, George Washington left office. He'd served two terms as president, and refused to run for a third. Who was elected second president of the United States? None other than John Adams.

John Adams was nervous about continuing with his son's appointment. After all, the 1796 election had been brutal, and going through with sending John Quincy to Lisbon could have given his enemies political ammunition to use against him.

*Portrait of 28-year-old John Quincy Adams in 1796
by John Singleton Copley.[2]*

He did it anyway. He almost gave in to the pressure he was under, but then he received a letter from George Washington. The letter urged him to "not withhold merited promotion for Mr. John [Quincy] Adams because he is your son." Washington went on to claim, "…Mr. Adams is the most valuable public character we have abroad" (Lincoln).

Then Comes Marriage

John Quincy left The Hague to go to London. On July 26, 1797, he kissed the bride. He and Louisa honeymooned on the English countryside. Three months later, the happy couple (and Thomas) left England.

However, they didn't go to Portugal. John Adams had sent his son a letter stating that, instead of Lisbon, he was to go to Berlin and serve as minister to Prussia. John Adams' political enemies caused him as much grief as they could over him giving such an important office to his son. The Senate delayed making a decision on John Quincy's appointment three times before finally confirming it.

So, on November 7, the Adamses arrived in Berlin and John Quincy assumed his role as minister. Life was good for a little while.

Then, Louisa miscarried. The young couple was crushed. When she miscarried again, they were devastated. Losing two children within a span of six months was a massive blow. John Quincy tended to his wife as best he could. He sat at her bedside. He offered words of comfort. But even a man of many words like him knew that they were powerless.

Louisa's depression seemed overwhelming. She was near the brink. But she did what survivors do. She survived. She survived one second, one hour, and one day at a time until the pain became bearable.

But, aside from the miscarriages, Mister and Misses Adams managed to enjoy the life they shared. As foreign officials, they spent their time among the upper class of Prussian society. They had a full social calendar, which mostly consisted of dinners and dances.

What was Louisa really like?
Louisa shined at social events. She held her own among Berlin's social elite to the point that her intelligence may have intimidated her husband. He worried that a direct, assertive woman like Louisa might speak out of turn and embarrass him. This fear turned out to be unfounded.

The Quasi-War

His active social life didn't keep John Quincy away from his more serious duties. He used Berlin as a listening post, and what he heard wasn't good. France had declared that it had a natural right to rule the world. To that end, it was preparing for more war. John Quincy sent report after report to the United States detailing what he believed the French to be planning. He had, as George Washington predicted, become his country's most valuable official abroad.

France's threats hadn't been empty. Shortly after John Quincy signed a trade deal with Prussia, French troops invaded Italy, Switzerland, the Rhineland, the Ionian Islands, and Dalmatia. French ships began capturing American merchant ships. Soon, more than half of the United States' merchant fleet was seized. All signs pointed to a war between America and France. (In fact, the situation would later be referred to as the Quasi-War.)

John Adams, always favoring neutrality like his son, didn't want that to happen. However, he knew that if it did, the USA had to be prepared. That meant assembling an army and a navy. He called 80,000 soldiers to active duty and ordered the construction of a dozen frigates.

John Adams also pursued diplomacy, but negotiating with the French was complicated by the XYZ Affair. Three French officials, then known only as X, Y, and Z, refused to hold peace talks with United States officials unless they agreed to pay a bribe to France. This offer was rejected.

There were congressmen who didn't believe that the XYZ Affair was real. They thought that anti-French politicians had made it up as an excuse to avoid signing a treaty with France.

A cartoon depicting the XYZ affair from 1799 showing Hydra-headed French government demanding money from Americans while armed with daggers.[3]

Documents were released by John Quincy that proved that the affair had happened. He also revealed the identities of X, Y, and Z to be Jean Conrad Hottinger, Monsieur Bellamy, and Lucien Hauteval. They had been acting under the orders of French minister Charles Talleyrand.

When the American public learned about the XYZ Affair, anger toward France boiled over. Towns across the nation formed militia groups ready to fight the French if necessary.

At first glance, the idea of going to war with France seemed insane. French troops and ships massively outnumbered American forces. But the tides of war were turning. Within a few months after being formed, the United States Navy captured more than 80 French ships.

France's luck soured elsewhere, too. Napoleon's invasion of Egypt had failed, and the embarrassing defeat sent shock waves through the diplomatic world, shock waves that knocked Talleyrand right off his feet.

John Quincy monitored the impact of the French defeat from his listening post in Berlin. He realized that France's loss would force it back to the negotiating table. "The present situation of the affairs of France… [has] produced a great and important change in her conduct toward us," he wrote in a letter to his father (Adams).

Finally, at the Convention of 1800, a deal was reached. French attacks on American shipping would stop. France would release American prisoners, and trade between the two countries, which had been interrupted by the conflict, would resume.

Fatherhood

1801 was a big year for John Quincy and Louisa. After four miscarriages and the heart-crushing suffering that went along with each of them, Louisa gave birth to a healthy baby boy. They welcomed their first-born child into the world on April 21 and named him George Washington Adams. It was a bold name, a combination of the United States' first two presidents.

At his son's baptism, John Quincy prayed that his son would "never be unworthy of it."

A few days later, John Quincy received the letter of recall that he'd been expecting. He could take his family home to the United States.

But what would he do once they got there?

Sources

1   Photo Credit: Everett Historical / Shutterstock.com
2   Photo Credit: Everett Historical / Shutterstock.com
3   Photo Credit: Everett Historical / Shutterstock.com

Chapter 9: Stateside Again

Looking for a Place in the World

On June 17, 1801, John Quincy, his wife, and his infant son left Berlin. They arrived in Hamburg, boarded a ship named *America*, and departed for Philadelphia. On September 4, their feet touched American soil. Their journey across the Atlantic had been, to their relief, uneventful. From Philadelphia, Louisa and her son traveled to Washington, D.C. to visit her parents. John Quincy stayed behind.

About a week later, John Quincy left Philadelphia to return to Quincy. He arrived on September 21 and reunited with his parents. He then set to work figuring out how to support his new family. With limited options, he decided to open another legal practice. The prospect of being a lawyer again didn't appeal to him at all, but he felt he had no other choice.

After purchasing and moving into a home in Boston, he wrote to Louisa, telling her about his recent decisions. He then went to Washington, D.C. to escort his wife and son to Boston. While in Washington, he visited Thomas Jefferson, who'd defeated

John Adams in the 1800 presidential election to become the third President of the United States. Despite that, and despite John Quincy's essay attacking Jefferson, the two got along well. Their old friendship was rekindled.

The family of three returned to Boston, and John Quincy resumed his career as a lawyer. He discovered that he hated it just as much as before and quickly found himself miserable. This left John Quincy with two options.

He could either find a new career … or stay miserable.

Vote Adams!

In 1802, John Quincy decided to run for a seat in the Massachusetts Senate. To his utter shock, he won easily. (He'd entered the election believing that his chance of winning was almost nothing.)

After taking his oath of office on May 26, John Quincy got to work. He fought to free the court system of Massachusetts from the authority of the Senate. He failed. He opposed the efforts of other Senators to create a new bank that would exist only to funnel money into their own pockets. He failed again.

John Quincy soon gained a reputation in the Massachusetts Senate for being honest, direct, and free-thinking. As those were hardly political qualities, his fellow Senators decided to get rid of him.

And they knew the perfect way to do it.

The Young Senator

Back in those days, congressional senators weren't elected by the public. They were appointed by their respective state senates. The Massachusetts Senators wanted John Quincy gone, and they couldn't fire him. So they did the next best thing — they promoted him.

John Quincy was to go to Washington to represent the people of Massachusetts. It was a huge honor. And an ironic one. Shortly after being elected to the Massachusetts Senate, he'd tried to run for a seat in the House of Representatives, but he lost to Dr. William Eustis. Now, John Quincy was being given a more important position, and he didn't have to run for office to win it.

On July 4, 1803, Louisa gave birth again. She named her second son John Adams II, in honor of her father-in-law. Two months later, John Quincy and Louisa left Boston for Washington D.C., taking their sons with them.

Life in the nation's capital was not pleasant. The city was barely developed, and most of the houses were nothing more than shacks. Many government officials lived in property outside of the city, as the city itself was little more than a poverty-stricken, rat-infested bog.

Fast Fact: John Quincy and his family stayed in a mansion. It was owned by his brother-in-law, Walter Hellen, who'd made a fortune in the tobacco industry.

After settling in, John Quincy got to work and found it quite easy. The Senate was only in session for two or three hours a day on weekdays. This left him time to read, write, and raise his children.

A major political debate was underway at the time. Thomas Jefferson was trying to make the Louisiana Purchase, which would double the size of the United States. This decision angered the people of New England. They saw that the economic potential of the new land was massive. Settlers planned to move there and build huge farms with slave labor. Those farms would out-produce and undersell New England farms, driving them out of business.

Furthermore, Jefferson didn't have the legal authority needed to make the Louisiana Purchase. The Constitution didn't allow the government to buy land. John Quincy realized this, but he also realized how good the Louisiana Purchase was for the United States. He rose to Jefferson's defense, arguing that buying the land was legal as long as the bill of purchase included the word "treaty," as the Constitution granted the government authority to make treaties. His argument was weak, but his skill in presenting it was strong enough to convince the Senate to go along with the purchase.

This surprised and delighted Jefferson. John Quincy, at that time, belonged to the Federalist Party, which opposed Jefferson's Democratic-Republican Party on most issues. However, John Quincy refused to bend to the will of either party. He voted with the Federalists against granting Jefferson the authority to tax the people of the Louisiana territory. After hours of debate on the Senate floor, votes were cast, and the Federalists were defeated.

As a result of his refusal to play into party politics, John Quincy once again gained a reputation for being honest, direct, and free-thinking. He expected this to lead to his political downfall but didn't waste time worrying about it.

He had other concerns.

Professor Adams

Harvard's faculty was looking for someone to serve as the college's first Professor of Rhetoric and Oratory. John Quincy was offered the honor. After working out a schedule that would allow him to meet his obligations in Congress, he was thrilled to accept.

Rhetoric and oratory, the skills he used every time he defended a political cause in the Senate, were near and dear to his heart.

His inspiration, as always, was Cicero, the Greek orator and philosopher. For part of his curriculum, John Quincy bought copies of Cicero's *Orations*. He also bought works by Aristotle, another noted Greek philosopher.

His salary at Harvard was $348 per quarter. He would start the following year, in 1808. In the meantime, his third son, Charles Francis Adams was born on August 18.

John Quincy, now forty years old, had lived out half of his life. His accomplishments included finishing second in his class at Harvard, serving as diplomat to two European nations, and serving as a Massachusetts Senator and as a U.S. Senator (where his skills as a speaker helped Jefferson double the size of the United States).

These seem like great achievements, and indeed they are, but they're dwarfed by what John Quincy would accomplish in the second half of his life.

As a Harvard professor, John Quincy delivered lectures focusing on ancient oratory and its relevance to modern politics. His lectures would later be compiled into a book, titled *Lectures on Rhetoric and Oratory*.

However, John Quincy felt that his own skills as an orator were lacking. "I was," he complained in his diary after a long day in Congress, "as I always am, miserably defective" (Adams).

Likely, his defectiveness had nothing to do with his skills as an orator, and everything to do with his refusal to blindly follow the will of either party.

John Quincy's enemies finally got their way. On June 8, 1808, he left the world of politics. This came after his fellow Massachusetts Federalists appointed James Lloyd to succeed him, a move that offended John Quincy greatly. Disgusted with the Federalists, the Democratic-Republicans, and the Senate itself, he chose to resign the remainder of his term.

Once again, John Quincy was faced with the prospect of life in the private sector. With his Harvard professorship, he had the means to support himself and his family. He reopened his legal practice, and it was much more successful than before. He still wasn't happy, though. He'd hoped to accomplish great things in Washington and that hope, in his mind at least, had been crushed.

John Adams wasn't surprised to learn that his son had lost his Senate seat. "You have too honest a heart, too independent a mind, and too brilliant talents..." John Adams wrote. He went on to encourage John Quincy to forget about politics and focus on his professorship, his career as a lawyer, and his family.

With the bitterness of defeat fresh in his mouth, John Quincy refused when Democratic-Republicans urged him to join their party and run for office in the Massachusetts Senate.

President Madison was sworn in as the fourth President of the United States on March 4, 1809. Shortly after taking office, he asked John Quincy to serve as minister to Russia. John Quincy accepted the offer without discussing it with anyone, including his wife.

Louisa was furious. She didn't want to leave the United States or be separated from her husband by over 4,000 miles. John Quincy's letter to Louisa explained his reasoning. "My personal motives for staying at home are of the strongest kind: the age of my parents and the infancy of my children… To oppose all this, I have the duty of a citizen to obey the call of his country…"

After giving his final lecture at Harvard, and saying goodbye to his students, whom he called his "unfailing friends," John Quincy made preparations to go to Saint Petersburg (Adams).

Given the harshness of the Russian climate, and the fact that he was unlikely to find any teachers who spoke English, he and Louisa decided to leave their two oldest boys behind and placed them in the care of relatives.

Chapter 10: Minister to Russia

Adams the Ambassador

On August 5, 1809, John Quincy, Louisa, and the infant Charles Francis boarded the *Horace,* a ship bound for Saint Petersburg. They arrived safely on October 13. Just a day later, the Russian winter set in, burying the city in a deep freeze.

John Quincy moved his family into an apartment, and despite the chilling weather, they settled into their new lives without much difficulty.

Thirty years earlier, Francis Dana and John Quincy had failed miserably in their diplomatic mission to Saint Petersburg, as Russian officials had refused to even meet them. As a result, John Quincy was doubtlessly nervous about how he would be received. Luckily for him, Russia had changed a lot in those years, and he found himself welcomed by the Russian court.

However, no one was more welcoming than Russian Emperor Alexander I.

John Quincy got along well with the well-mannered, educated ruler, and their initially political relationship soon evolved into a genuine friendship. Alexander and John Quincy, who spoke to each other mostly in French, took daily walks (despite the cold) and discussed a variety of topics, from international news to American fashion.

John Quincy's post in Russia brought him into contact with officials from several European nations, including France, Spain, Holland, Prussia, and Sweden. Taking advantage of this, he sent reports regarding the affairs of most of Europe back to the United States.

In the early 1800s, the chief concern of all of Europe could have been summarized in one word: Napoleon.

The charisma, military genius, and lust for power of Napoleon Bonaparte had led to his conquering a huge portion of Europe. His kingdom, including puppet governments, stretched across more than 2,000 miles. Was that enough for him?

John Quincy didn't think so. He knew that Napoleon was a threat to the world, and a great deal of the information he in gathered while in Russia was regarding the French dictator.

But, unfortunately, the French Empire wasn't the only thing John Quincy had to worry about.

*Emperor Napoleon Bonaparte painted
by Baron François Gerard in the early 1800s.[1]*

The Air of Heaven

John Quincy enjoyed life in Russia. He enjoyed it so much that, when James Madison nominated him to the United States Supreme Court, he turned it down.

But sadly, life in Russia was about to get a lot more difficult. Louisa was pregnant again and the threat of miscarriage hung over her head like the blade of a guillotine. Because she had already miscarried twice since arriving in Russia, John Quincy and Louisa prepared for the worst.

Only the worst didn't happen — not at first. On August 11, 1810, Louisa gave birth to a baby girl. She named her first and only daughter Louisa Catherine Adams. She and John Quincy were overjoyed to have been blessed by her.

The blessing did not last long. Dysentery, an infection of the intestines, was common in the area. Shortly before her first birthday, Louisa Catherine was struck by it.

On September 15, 1811, John Quincy wrote in his diary, "At twenty-five minutes past one this morning expired my daughter, Louisa Catherine, as lovely an infant as ever breathed the air of Heaven."

Having lost her two-month battle with dysentery, Louisa Catherine was buried in the graveyard of the same Anglican church where she'd been baptized.

Where Invasions Go to Die

Napoleon Bonaparte wasn't afraid of the climate of Russia, or dysentery, or any of the other challenges that the enormous country presented. On June 24, 1812, he began his invasion of Russia.

The French army of 450,000 soldiers marched across hundreds of miles without encountering much resistance from the Russians. But, they did encounter resistance from Russia itself. Within two months, Napoleon had lost over 100,000 men to starvation and sickness.

Then they approached Moscow.

On September 7, 1812, the Imperial Russian Army collided with Napoleon's forces in the Battle of Borodino. It was the bloodiest battle of the war. Napoleon lost between 30,000 and 35,000 men. The Russians lost between 40,000 and 45,000 men. The Russians also lost the battle itself, and retreated, leaving the city of Moscow to Napoleon.

Capturing Moscow felt like a victory to Napoleon. But his men felt defeated. Months of grueling travel were taking its toll.

It was a toll Napoleon couldn't afford. He paid it anyway.

At least, his men did. Napoleon had won the battle but was losing the war. The Russians employed a scorched-earth strategy, destroying useful resources before they retreated, leaving the French with nothing left to forage. Soon, the French were starving. To make matters worse, they were being attacked on all sides by Russian cavalry. Cossacks, people from southern Russia who were known for their ability to fight on horseback, launched countless hit-and-run attacks on Napoleon's army, wearing it down more and more.

To make matters worse, winter was setting in. As the temperature dropped, so did Napoleon's chances of victory.

After a series of smaller battles, Napoleon realized that he had no hope of wiping out the Russian army. He gave the order to retreat. Of the nearly half-million men who invaded Russia, only about 20,000 escaped the country alive.

In Saint Petersburg, John Quincy and his family were safe. He spent his days learning what he could about the war to report to the United States. Napoleon's defeat, and the slaughter of his army during its retreat convinced John Quincy more than ever that, for the U.S. to survive, it needed to stay neutral in European affairs.

But it didn't. In fact, the U.S. had recently declared war with Britain. The War of 1812, which, despite its name, lasted almost three years. It began in June, the same month Napoleon launched his doomed invasion.

The idea that the U.S. was at war with a country as powerful as Britain was terrifying. Could the 36-year-old republic survive another war with the most powerful nation on earth?

And, after so many years of bad blood between the two countries, what would it take to restore peace between them? Nothing short of a miracle.

Sources
1   Photo Credit: Everett – Art / Shutterstock.com

Chapter 11: The Treaty of Ghent

John Quincy Adams: Miracle Worker

The War of 1812 had multiple causes. Perhaps the biggest was that the British had used their navy to capture approximately 10,000 American sailors and forced them to work on their ships. Another was that British colonies in America were giving aid to American Indians who were at war with the United States.

The conflicts between the two nations had resulted in a trade embargo. This was hard on both nations' economies. Before the recent conflicts, Britain was the biggest buyer of the United States' raw materials, and the U.S. had been the biggest buyer of Britain's manufactured goods.

Britain, seeking to end the conflict, actually sent a ship to the United States bearing an offer to cease all acts of aggression and reopen trade. It was too late. While the ship was crossing the Atlantic, President James Madison declared war on England.

It didn't go well. The British troops won a series of battles along the northern frontier, capturing and killing American soldiers who were overwhelmed and undertrained.

At sea, however, the United States fared much better. Its tiny navy, which consisted of only a dozen ships, (all of them well-built, well-armed frigates) took on the vastly superior British fleet, inflicting losses off the coasts of Virginia, Nova Scotia, Brazil, and even Africa.

In addition to the dozen-frigate navy, the United States' campaign at sea was aided by approximately 500 privateer vessels that captured more than 1,300 British cargo vessels.

President Madison, having realized the danger the United States was in, tried to negotiate using his country's success at sea for leverage. It didn't work. The British were still bitter about the loss of the American colonies and hoped to regain them. They wanted to fight on.

John Quincy, aware that Russia was an ally of Britain, asked Alexander I to influence the British government to agree to peace. He tried.

But Britain still wanted to fight on. That is, until the United States started winning.

On April 27, 1813, American soldiers, led by General Henry Dearborn, sailed across Lake Ontario and defeated British forces in the city of York before plundering the city and setting it ablaze.

Dearborn's men then traveled west to join forces with Colonel Winfield Scott's army of 2,500. Winfield, true to his name, led his troops to victory, and captured Fort Niagara, Fort Erie, and Fort George.

On Lake Erie, American ships added to the winning streak by defeating the British navy in a costly battle. Captain Oliver Perry, who had a fleet of 10 ships under his command, crushed Britain's six frigates and earned himself the title "Hero of Lake Erie."

This painting from 1813 shows Commodore Perry during The Battle of Lake Erie.[1]

As America scored victory after victory and gained ground in the north, it scored political power and gained leverage against the British. They were no longer so eager to march to the beat of their own war drum. They were ready to talk peace.

President Madison was thrilled, and he knew that to have good negotiations, he'd need a good negotiator. And he had the best.

Back in Saint Petersburg, John Quincy had closely followed the ups and downs of the War of 1812. Finally, in 1814, he received a letter. He was to serve as head diplomat in peace talks with the British. If all went well, he'd be rewarded for his service by being appointed foreign minister to Britain.

On April 28, 1814, John Quincy left Russia without his wife and son, whom he didn't want to put at risk.

Around that time, a hybrid force of several European nations seized Paris and defeated Napoleon, capturing the former dictator.

This affected the situation between the United States and Britain because the 14,000 British troops Napoleon had been holding captive were released shortly after his defeat. These troops set sail for the United States, ready to battle.

And that's what they did. Raids and cannon fire devastated coastal cities in Virginia, Massachusetts, and Connecticut.

This happened despite peace talks that were scheduled to begin in the Belgian city of Ghent. Both sides wanted peace, but they both wanted it on their own terms. Each nation wanted to punish the other for perceived injustices, despite the economic and human costs of the war. United States and British leaders were hoping that, if war raged on, their side would score a decisive enough victory to force the other side to agree to peace under any terms necessary.

John Quincy reached Stockholm, Sweden, in late May. He arrived in Hamburg a few days later. On June 12, after enjoying a rest in the country he loved so much, he boarded the *USS John Adams* and set sail for Amsterdam. After arriving in Amsterdam, John Quincy began the trek to Ghent.

He had an abundance of free time during his travels. He used it to write letters to his wife, describing the sights and sounds of Europe as he traveled. He also described his feelings for her.

John Quincy wasn't the easiest person to be around. Being married to the man must have required massive patience on Louisa's part. Her husband, though never violent, was often cranky and sharp-tongued. He had a bad habit of keeping his love for his partner buried so deep in his heart that she may have doubted it existed at all. But it did. John Quincy, for all of his gruffness, loved his wife more than anything and being away from her pained him greatly.

An End to War

After arriving in Ghent, John Quincy waited for the talks to begin. Also waiting were the other four American diplomats: James A. Bayard, Henry Clay, Albert Gallatin, and Jonathan Russell.

The group, who'd been appointed by President Madison, had to wait until August 8 for the negotiations to start.

And they didn't start well.

The British wanted to keep the Americans they'd captured and forced to work as sailors. Of course, John Quincy and his fellow diplomats wouldn't stand for that.

They also wouldn't stand for the British demand to create a buffer state.

The idea of the buffer state was to stop the United States from growing. Many American officials, including John Quincy and Henry Clay, wanted their nation to expand westward. Britain wanted to stop that from happening, and believed that best way to do it was by helping American Indians form their own nation. The nation would have received supplies and military support from Britain, enabling the British to attack the United States easily.

When John Quincy and his comrades made it clear that the buffer state was an absolute deal-breaker, the British conceded. They agreed not to pursue the matter further.

However, they made two other bold demands that were shot down. They wanted Americans to surrender their naval presence on the Great Lakes. They also wanted the British colonies to be granted access to the Mississippi River. Negotiations broke down as a result.

Meanwhile, the war itself showed no sign of slowing down. American soldiers were defeated at Battle of Bladensburg in Maryland. The battle, which humiliated American soldiers, was later referred to as the Bladensburg races by the British. The battle marked the first time in history that American troops encountered rockets, a new invention. The explosions, which seemed to fall from Heaven itself, terrified them into retreat. And they retreated right through the heart of Washington D.C. itself.

The British then invaded the United States' capital city and set it ablaze. Luckily, a massive storm passed over the city, putting out the fires and allowing American forces to swiftly recapture it.

As the war raged on, the months dragged on. John Quincy grew more and more frustrated with himself, his colleagues, and the British. The recent humiliation of American forces made the idea of a treaty seem almost out of the question. British officials, realizing they had the upper hand, refused to back down from most of their previous demands.

But, when the outcomes of the battles in America started changing, so did the attitudes of the British diplomats. The Battle of Baltimore, in which the British attempted to capture the economically vital trade city in Maryland, ended in a decisive American victory. British troops, overwhelmed by American forces at land and sea, retreated. Furthermore, Robert Ross, the British commander who had given the order to set fire to Washington D.C., was killed in the battle.

British victory once again seemed uncertain, perhaps unlikely. Since the war with Napoleon had ended, the British agreed to end the practice of impressment and remove trade restrictions with the United States. It was an important step toward peace.

But it was just a step. Everything else was at a standstill. To the negotiators in Ghent, every day was a verbal Tug of War. Both sides tried to use recent defeats and victories for leverage, resulting in a seemingly endless war of words.

At the forefront of this was John Quincy. He prided himself on his skills as a speaker, but the unending months of monotonous debate wore his patience thin. His relationships with the other American diplomats became strained. All five of them began to bicker on a daily basis about how to handle talks with the British.

Luckily, the two nations were as tired of war as the negotiators were of negotiating. After five months of bitter argument, something shocking happened — progress. It was finally being made!

This print from 1815 symbolizes the peace achieved by the Treaty of Ghent. This shows Minerva, the goddess of war, wisdom, art, schools and commerce, dictating the terms of peace. Mercury is shown delivering them to Britannia, the female personification of the island of Britain. Hercules compels Britannia to accept.[2]

Both sides realized that the cost of war wasn't worth paying. It had taken more than two years — two bloody, costly years — for them to come to this conclusion.

Finally, the British and the Americans agreed.

To nothing.

There were no significant changes in territory and neither side had really won anything. At the end of the conflict, no one had anything to show for it. The war that had begun as a mistake was finally being rectified.

For Americans and Brits, Christmas came early that year. The Treaty of Ghent was signed on December 24, 1814. The governments of both nations would provide approval.

And, just like that, the war was basically over.

But not quite. While the news of peace traveled across the Atlantic by boat, the War of 1812 dragged on into 1815. And it was only getting bloodier.

General Andrews Jackson, known for his fiercely aggressive personality, led Americans troops in the Battle of New Orleans.

British troops, numbering approximately 11,000, wanted to capture the strategically significant city. They faced an army of fewer than 5,000 Americans.

On paper, the Americans looked outmatched. But, on the battlefield, it was a different story.

A painting of Andrew Jackson at The Battle of New Orleans.[3]

The Battle of New Orleans didn't turn out to be so much a battle as a one-sided beating. And it lasted for 10 days, from January 8 to January 18. During the battle, British troops, acting under the command of General Edward Pakenham, stormed the city. At least, they tried to storm the city. Andrew Jackson, his men, and their cannons wouldn't allow it. It took massive bravery for the British to attack, knowing that their enemies were prepared for them. But bravery alone doesn't stop cannonballs or bullets.

Between those killed, wounded, and captured, the British casualties numbered more than 2,000. How many casualties did the Americans suffer? About 60. And no, that isn't a typo. American casualties really were only 0.03 percent of British casualties.

When news of the peace treaty arrived, both sides, exhausted from conflict, celebrated. The war that shouldn't have happened, the war that had accomplished nothing, was finally over.

John Quincy's job was done, and his reward was well-deserved.

Sources

1   Photo Credit: Everett Historical / Shutterstock.com
2   Photo Credit: Library of Congress / Engraver: Alexis Chataigner / Artist: Julia Plantou
     / Created by: Philadelphia : P. Price, Jr. / Control Number: 2003670665
3   Photo Credit: Everett Historical / Shutterstock.com

Chapter 12: The Court of Saint James

A Terrifying Journey

Since he'd successfully negotiated the Treaty of Ghent, John Quincy was appointed minister to Britain, the most important overseas role his country had to offer. Although he'd already become the United States' most valued public official abroad, (as predicted by Washington) the appointment to England made it official.

John Quincy wrote to his wife, saying, "…come with Charles to me at Paris, where I shall be impatiently waiting for you. I calculate upon your receiving this letter about the twentieth of January, and I suppose you will not be able to make all the necessary arrangements to leave St. Petersburg sooner than the middle of February" (Adams).

But she did leave Saint Petersburg sooner than the middle of February. She and Charles left on January 26, after selling most of the family's possessions in Russia and arranging for the rest to be shipped to England.

The Journey from Saint Petersburg to Paris was terrifying. The chaos from Napoleon's defeat hadn't completely died down. The rotting bodies of soldiers and horses were still strewn along the roads. And there were bandits.

The bandits were mostly soldiers, survivors of the Franco-Russian War who had no way home and could only make a living by highway robberies.

When he learned about incidents taking place along the roads that Louisa and Charles would be traveling, John Quincy regretted his decision to call her to Paris. He nervously awaited their arrival, hoping and praying for their safety.

Louisa and Charles traveled in a carriage with a nurse. Behind them trailed a second carriage containing two servants.

Everything went smoothly at first. Then they got lost near Mitau, Latvia. They spent the evening wandering obscure backroads, wondering if they should turn back or keep pressing on.

They chose to keep going. Louisa wrote, "We were jolted over hills, through swamps, and holes and into valleys into which no carriage had surely ever passed before, and my whole heart was filled with unspeakable horrors for the safety of my child" (Traub).

The situation must have seemed hopeless to her. She was lost and defenseless, deep in the heart of a foreign country where she didn't speak the language, doing little more than waiting to be found by bandits.

But bandits didn't find Louisa's group. A farmer did. And he was friendly enough to direct them back to civilization.

They found their way to Prussia and expected to travel from there on without incident. They weren't so lucky. A broken wheel delayed their journey by almost a day. Then they traveled through Leipzig. The experience was horrifying.

The Battle of Leipzig, in which Napoleon's retreating army had been crushed, was, at the time, the biggest battle in European history. Nearly 100,000 soldiers had died and many of their bodies remained, having rotted into skeletons.

But scarier than the dead French soldiers was the threat of living ones. Rumors reached Louisa that Napoleon had escaped captivity and returned to power. The political climate in France had changed again. She knew what that meant. The border to France could be closed by the time her group reached it. Or worse, her group might be attacked.

And, making a bad situation worse, her two servants refused to go to the French border. They were afraid of being drafted into the French army.

After hiring a 14-year-old boy to drive the carriage that her two servants had been in charge of, she carried on.

They arrived at the French border. To her infinite joy, it had not been closed. Louisa and company traveled on toward Paris.

Her two-carriage caravan was about halfway between the French border and Paris when they encountered a group of French soldiers that was on its way to join Napoleon. The soldiers greeted them with a cry: "Tear them out of the carriage. They are Russians, take them out and kill them" (Traub).

With rifles pointed at her head, Louisa explained calmly in French that she was not only an American, but the wife of John Quincy Adams. Luckily, the soldiers believed her. She and her group were allowed to live.

Two days later, they arrived in Paris.

Louisa and John Quincy were reunited. When she recounted her 40-day journey to him, he was stunned. First, he was stunned by his wife's bravery. Second, he was stunned that he'd been foolish enough to allow her to travel under such circumstances.

Louisa, however, showed no signs of anger or bitterness. She was simply happy to have the family reunited and finally on its way to London.

Off to England

When Louisa reached Paris, the papers for John Quincy's position in Britain had not yet arrived. Refusing to leave for London until everything was in order, the Adamses stayed in Paris.

They saw the sights, sampled the food, and enjoyed the theater. They even explored the famous catacombs of Paris, where millions of skeletons were said to be housed.

And, speaking of dead, Napoleon arrived in Paris with a massive army in March. Soldiers who'd been sent by French King Louis XVIII to capture Napoleon had instead joined him, swelling his ranks significantly. By June, he would be able to field more than 200,000 troops. John Quincy didn't have to wait that long.

In May, he, Louisa, and Charles left Paris. They traveled 40 miles to the Marquis de Lafayette's castle. The castle, known as Château de la Grange-Bléneau, which dated back to the 12th century, was a remarkable sight. The company was remarkable, too.

John Quincy and the Marquis de Lafayette's friendship was a warm one. They were two icons of two generations, both of whom shaped the early history of America.

After four days of reminiscing, John Quincy, having finally received his necessary paperwork, departed with his family to travel to London.

Leaving France was complicated, considering the thousands of Napoleon-fearing people who were trying to do the same.

At the port of Le Havre, the Adamses managed to secure passage on a Danish ship. They departed on May 23, the same day that the French declared martial law and closed off all ports.

Having escaped being trapped in France, the Adamses traveled across the English Channel through fierce weather. The voyage, though it only took a day, was hard on the three of them. Seasickness made their experience miserable.

They arrived in Britain and set off for London. On the way, they were harassed by a low-ranking government official who accused the two of smuggling silk into Britain. John Quincy produced his passport, which had been signed by Lord Castlereagh. The official, realizing how much John Quincy outranked him in terms of social status, blurted out an apology before scurrying away.

The Adams trio arrived in London on the evening of May 25. They were reunited with John Adams II and George Washington Adams, who'd crossed the Atlantic under the care of two Americans, Edward Everett and George Ticknor. It was the first time the family had been together in six years.

And that wasn't the only reunion. Two of John Quincy's subordinates from the signing of the Treaty of Ghent were in London: Henry Clay and Albert Gallatin. They were negotiating a trade agreement with the British.

Despite decades of bad blood between the two nations, the economic fates of the U.S. and Britain were bound together. In the years leading up to the War of 1812, trade between the two nations had been critical to both. The United States was rich with raw materials and Britain, among the most technologically advanced nations in the world, could supply manufactured goods to the United States.

John Quincy, among the most gifted orators alive, could have played a big role in negotiating the new trade deal. At least, he could have if there had been anything left to negotiate. His delay in leaving France had resulted in him being left out of most of the debating process.

John Quincy supervised the remainder of the negotiations. The British officials took on a new air of confidence when Napoleon's brief return to power came to an end after the Battle of Waterloo. The French dictator's defeat removed a significant threat to Britain and freed up its military resources. Luckily, the talks still went smoothly.

Once the deal was signed, John Quincy had even less to do. As prestigious as his new job was, it was effectively part-time.

A New Lust for Life

Shortly after arriving in Britain, John Quincy moved his family out of London. They went to stay in the nearby village of Ealing, where housing was much cheaper.

Now in his mid-forties, John Quincy had spent his entire adult life (and most of his childhood) working tirelessly. For the first time in a long time, he could slow down and savor life at a more leisurely pace.

He and Louisa, now that they were with their children and far away from the French army, were happier than they'd been in a long time.

There was only one problem. As much as John Quincy loved his two oldest sons and enjoyed having them with him, he found their education severely lacking. He was especially disappointed in his oldest son's shortcomings. George Washington Adams, now 14 years old, was nowhere near prepared to attend Harvard like his father, grandfather, and great-grandfather before him.

John Quincy enrolled John and Charles Francis in boarding school and focused on properly educating his oldest son. George hated every second of it. John Quincy required him to rise from bed before six in the morning and begin studying at once. To his father's frustration, he refused.

When he did get up, he was immediately set to work studying Latin, Greek, and French. A particular challenge was when his father made him translate passages of Cicero to and from Latin.

John Quincy enjoyed being a teacher, but George hated being his student. After massive amounts of begging and pleading, John Quincy relented. To his disappointment, his oldest son didn't aspire to be a world leader or political figure of any kind.

With his father's reluctant permission, George left his father's home to tour Europe by himself.

Surprisingly, John Quincy's good spirits persisted. He realized that his oldest son wasn't going to be following in his footsteps. He wasn't thrilled with that, but he accepted it.

His newfound lust for life grew stronger. He discovered that he enjoyed working as minister to Britain. There wasn't much for him to do in his office on Craven Street and he had two secretaries to help him do it. His official duties, which were mostly limited to signing passports and paying attention to international news, only took up a few hours a day. That left him with plenty of free time. Time was an increasingly precious commodity to the man now in the second half of his life. He spent much of it with Louisa, Charles Francis, and John Adams II.

John Quincy's new lease on life served him well as minister to Britain. He became well-liked by the Court of Saint James, Britain's royal court. Government officials, including Prime Minister Robert Jenkinson himself, were impressed by the education and social graces of the balding, heavy-set American.

His social life became active. Extravagant dinners and parties took up many of his evenings. Had he not mellowed, he probably would have found these events annoying. Those were his usual feelings at previous events in Prussia, Russia, and the Netherlands. But he shined at them. He came into contact with many powerful people, including the Duke of Wellington.

Wellington had led coalition forces to victory against Napoleon at the Battle of Waterloo. This made him a hero throughout most of Europe. He and John Quincy got along fine, as John Quincy found it amusing that the Duke often had trouble staying awake into the evening. He often yawned loudly while at the dinner table.

John Quincy also became acquainted with Sir Matthew Wood, the mayor of London, William IV, the duke of Clarence, and Robert Stewart (usually known as Lord Castlereagh) the Leader of the House of Commons.

John Quincy and Louisa enjoyed the dinners, dances, balls, and celebrations in London (despite being expected to host a few themselves, which John Quincy's low salary made difficult).

But John Quincy's good times in Britain nearly came to a fatal end.

One day, he decided to teach his two youngest sons how to use pistols. The problem was, he barely knew how to use them himself. He mistakenly loaded powder into the same gun twice. When he fired it, the pistol should have exploded in his hand, spraying a lethal dose of wood, metal, fire, and gunpowder into the face of the future president.

It didn't.

Somehow, he wasn't fatally injured. The pistol didn't explode, at least not fully. It burst into flames and flew out of his grip. An incident that could have easily killed him only ended up burning his hand and eyes and wounding his pride.

It was around that time that a storm cloud of depression smothered John Quincy's sunny outlook on life. It came almost out of nowhere. Writer's block set in, which ground his journaling and letter writing to a screeching halt. And his social graces left too. He lost all desire for human interaction, except with Louisa.

The injuries caused by the misfire seemed to have triggered the return of his pessimistic outlook on life, but the negativity would persist even after the wounds had healed.

His only joy in life was Louisa who read to him every day while he was recovering. He would lie in bed, eyes closed, listening to his wife's angelic voice as she read him the works of Sir Walter Scott and Maria Edgeworth.

After he regained full use of his eyes and the pain in his hand subsided, he began, ever so slowly, to rejoin the world. He resumed correspondence with his parents. He resumed his job as minister, and, for the first time since the explosion, he seemed OK again.

But only OK. Never, in the remainder of his life, would John Quincy be as happy and carefree and he'd been those first few months in Britain.

Part 3: A Leader

At this point in his story, John Quincy Adams had already made quite a mark on the world. He'd served as minister to four European nations. He'd played a decisive role in convincing Congress to make the Louisiana Purchase, and he'd led the negotiations that resulted in the Treaty of Ghent.

As a younger man, he'd shown a massive amount of promise. And, as an older man, he'd lived up to all of it.

Throughout his career, he'd made friends and enemies in high places. There were people who respected him for his directness, honesty, and refusal to compromise his beliefs. And there were people who hated him for the same reasons.

John Quincy's time overseas was almost at an end. Back in the United States, two very important offices were waiting for him.

Chapter 13: Appointed Secretary

Family Matters

On March 4, 1817, James Monroe took office as the fifth President of the United States. At the time, the nation was enjoying the "Era of Good Feelings." With the War of 1812 having come to a close, and trade relations with Britain strengthening the United States' economy, Americans were optimistic and united.

Their optimism and unity reached Washington. Monroe, putting pragmatism over party politics, made presidential cabinet appointments based on merit alone. Therefore, John Quincy was offered an important position: secretary of state. This was despite the notion that Monroe was a Republican and John Quincy was a Federalist. However, their worldviews were similar.

Portrait of President James Monroe by Gilbert Stuart in 1817.[1]

The secretary of state oversaw the State Department, which dealt with foreign affairs. It was the traditional stepladder to the presidency.

John Quincy hesitated. Despite everything he'd accomplished so far, he doubted himself. He wasn't sure that he, with his lack of patience, had the temperament for the position. "I had no expectation, or belief, that the office would be offered to me... A doubt of my competency for it is very sincerely entertained, and ought perhaps to be decisive" (Adams).

Louisa disagreed. She believed in her husband and encouraged him to accept the appointment.

And, after giving it more thought, he did. He and Louisa began preparations to return to the United States.

John and Abigail Adams, now elderly, had feared they wouldn't live to see their son again. They were thrilled when they learned that he was coming home.

On June 15, John Quincy, Louisa, and their three sons set sail for home. John Quincy predicted that he was leaving Britain for the last time. He was right.

He brought along pieces of furniture that he'd acquired in Britain and Russia. He also brought his massive library. Unfortunately, his wine collection, which numbered 858 bottles, had to be left behind.

Stormy seas made the voyage miserable enough for everyone, but John Quincy made himself more miserable by losing numerous games of chess to fellow passengers. His defeats angered him greatly. He hated losing, and began spending a great deal of his time studying the game. He read books about chess strategy that he acquired from the ship's library, but his skill only improved slightly.

His 50th birthday came. The bad weather let up that day, as if nature itself respected the future president. The crew and other passengers congratulated John Quincy and threw him a party of sorts. There was no cake or candles, but there was plenty of drinking and songs sung in John Quincy's honor.

On August 6, the ship arrived in New York City. It was the first time John Quincy had returned to the United States in eight years. He would never leave again.

The Adamses spent 10 days relaxing in New York City before departing for Quincy. On August 18, they arrived in the city of John Quincy's birth.

John Quincy was thrilled. So were his parents. Their oldest son and his wife had returned with their children. The grandparents marveled at how their grandsons had grown while overseas.

The next three weeks were a social whirlwind. Politicians crawled out of the woodwork to befriend the new secretary of state. John Quincy found himself being dragged to dinner parties, balls, and other social events that he found boring.

Finally, the welcome wagon stopped, allowing him to focus on more serious matters.

Despite his previous contentment with his son's lack of interest in higher education, John Quincy wanted to enroll George in Harvard.

So George applied and, to no one's surprise, he was rejected. John Quincy then arranged for George to live in Cambridge and receive tutoring. His other two sons were sent to a boarding school in Boston.

George's education wasn't the only family matter that concerned John Quincy. His brother Tom had fallen victim to the family vice: alcoholism. The disease ran rampant through the men in Abigail Adams' side of the family. It had spared John Quincy (despite his love of wine) but Tom seemed helpless against it.

Alcoholism had already killed Charles Adams, and Nabby had died of cancer in 1813. Tom was the only sibling John Quincy had left, and he didn't want to lose him.

But this was before interventions, rehab clinics and 12-step programs. And John Quincy wasn't good at talking about his feelings.

So he focused on another issue: bookkeeping.

Tom had been trusted by his parents to run the family finances, which included several properties and investments. Fortunately, he hadn't run them into the ground. In fact, the estate under his control had grown to a net worth of over $100,000.

His bookkeeping practices, however, had been abysmal. John Quincy reviewed the records kept by his brother, finding them incomplete and disorganized. He made sense of what he could, but eventually gave up, regarding it as a lost cause. Luckily, the IRS didn't exist yet.

Then, after being back in the United States for not quite a month, John Quincy and Louisa departed for Washington D.C.

John Quincy still had doubts. He didn't know if he had what it took to be secretary of state. He had no idea he'd go down in history as one of the greatest ever.

A New Challenge

John Quincy and Louisa traveled to Washington D.C. by way of steamboat. It wasn't quite a new invention in 1817, but it was new to them. It cut their travel time down to a third of what it would have been had they taken a coach.

They arrived on September 17 and moved in with one of Louisa's sisters. They would stay there until they could arrange for permanent lodgings.

John Quincy met with President Monroe and his other appointees. Monroe was staying at 1600 Pennsylvania Ave., at a building that had been nicknamed "The White House" due to its recently added thick coat of white paint.

Among the other men offered positions in the president's cabinet was Henry Clay. Monroe had offered Clay, who was the speaker of the House of Representatives, the position of secretary of war. But being secretary of war in a time of peace wasn't an important position, certainly not the kind that would serve as a stepping-stone to the presidency. Clay refused the appointment.

He was more interested in John Quincy's office. He knew that, as secretary of state, John Quincy was a likely candidate to serve as the next president. Clay lusted after the presidency and decided to do everything within his power to sabotage John Quincy.

Shortly after John Quincy was appointed secretary, Clay convinced the House to cut the budget of the State Department. It was a disgusting tactic, and a blatantly obvious abuse of his power.

But he got away with it. The entire State Department, vital to the existence of the United States, was made to run on a starvation budget of approximately $125,000 per year. And John Quincy's salary was a puny $3,500 per year.

The State Department, that oversaw foreign relationships vital to maintaining peace, trade deals vital to the American economy, and matters pertaining to immigration, was running on 10 percent of the budget that similar departments in Europe were granted. But, somehow, John Quincy made it work.

Unfortunately, Clay wasn't John Quincy's only political enemy. Vice President Daniel D. Tompkins and Secretary of the Treasury William H. Crawford also despised him.

Crawford, the most juvenile of John Quincy's opposition, would often waste time at cabinet meetings making absurd proposals that the future president would have to waste time shooting down.

What the men opposing John Quincy's ascension to the presidency didn't realize was that, at that point, he wasn't interested in it. There's no evidence that John Quincy accepted the position of secretary of state with the idea of the presidency in mind, and there's abundant evidence against it. He told numerous family members and close friends that he didn't want the office. Considering the disgusting state of politics, he decision was understandable.

However, his opponents thought he was trying to lower their guard so he could outmaneuver them. The idea that he was an honest man who only wanted to do his job was inconceivable to them.

Luckily for John Quincy, President Monroe was on his side. The two got along well and Monroe became active in helping John Quincy run the State Department. Thomas Jefferson commented that, "Monroe showed his usual good sense in appointing Adams. They were made for each other. Adams has a pointed pen; Monroe has judgment enough for both and firmness enough to have his judgment control" (Lincoln).

Monroe agreed that the budget John Quincy was trying to work with was absurd, but, as president, there was nothing he could do about it. Later, in 1819, John Quincy was given some relief when Congress doubled his salary to $7,000 annually, but his yearly expenses still exceeded his income.

Despite this handicap, John Quincy was determined to do his job properly. He met foreign officials, advised American officials, and spent many stressful hours arguing with the other members of Monroe's cabinet. He also oversaw every detail when the State Department was moved into a new building.

Life wasn't any easier for Louisa. She found herself an outcast among the women of Washington's social elite. When she and John Quincy first moved to the city, the wives of senators and congressmen had expected her to stop by their homes and introduce herself to them. Since the roads in D.C. were little more than muddy ruts, Louisa couldn't bring herself to bother. Soon, the label of "snob" was seemingly tattooed on her public image. Rehabilitating her social standing wouldn't have mattered, but, within a year or so moving to D.C., the political games began to draw John Quincy in. Quietly, he began to entertain thoughts of running for president. And he had more than his fair share of supporters. Many people around him, and around the country, recognized his intelligence and dedication. Despite the best efforts of his enemies to smear him, he found himself positioned to run a strong campaign.

He stayed coy, sticking to the balance of duty and defiance that made him iconic. He no longer outright rejected the idea of running for president, but he refused to commit to it.

Louisa began doing damage control by hosting social events at the Adams household. John Quincy, well aware that he was seen by many as being smug and unfriendly, did his best to come across as likeable.

Meanwhile, he kept busy at his job. Britain and the United States had more business to discuss: territorial boundaries and access to fishing waters. Luckily, negotiations went smoothly. The resulting agreement, the Treaty of 1818, guaranteed the U.S. the right to fish along Newfoundland and Labrador, arranged for joint control of Oregon Country, and worked out the exact boundary where the U.S. ended and the British territories began.

John Quincy also kept busy with his poetry. He'd been composing verses for most of his life, but he was private about it. To him, poetry was an art that let him communicate his most personal thoughts. Here's one of them:

> Extend, all-seeing God, thy hand,
>   In mercy still decree,
> And make to bless my native land
>   An instrument of me.

His lifelong love of the written word gave him peace when the rest of his world was wrought with conflict. And, when the pressures of public service overwhelmed him, he dreamed of a career as an author. He continued make entries in his diary, expressing his frustration with the world of politics and his desire to get out of it for good.

It was a strange contradiction, wanting to leave his profession and rise to the top of it at the same time. Perhaps it made sense in his mind. If he felt he had to stay in politics because of his pride and sense of duty, he could at least bring his career to the perfect conclusion by holding the highest office in the land. Then he could retire to a solitary life of writing.

Or so he thought.

Defending Jackson

John Quincy didn't let his budding presidential aspirations or even his daydreams of being a full-time author distract him. He stayed focused on being the best secretary of state that he could be.

And it wasn't easy. A war was going on. It wasn't at the same level of intensity as the War of 1812, but John Quincy wanted to stop it before it could escalate. Escaped slaves and native tribes living in Spanish-controlled Florida had repeatedly launched quick, sneak-attack style raids into Georgia. General Andrew Jackson was put in charge of stopping the raids. Since he couldn't catch the attackers while they were in U.S. territory, he invaded Florida.

The settlements in Florida were caught completely off guard. Jackson's men marched from east to west Florida, destroying every Seminole fort and settlement they encountered.

And, to send a message, Jackson captured two Creek chiefs and hanged them in public view.

In late May, his army arrived in Pensacola. He'd ravaged the entire Florida panhandle. Then, making the situation even more dire, he captured two British merchants and had them publicly executed for aiding the enemy.

Monroe's entire cabinet condemned Jackson. So did the Spanish and British governments. Jackson had gone far beyond the scope of his original mission. His actions could have destroyed the United States' relationship with Spain and Britain, ruining critical trade agreements and even dragging the United States into further conflict. But John Quincy wasn't about to let that happen.

For someone as antisocial as John Quincy at times, he knew how to be persuasive when the mood struck him. He stood alone in Monroe's cabinet, defending Jackson's actions. He argued that the attacks on Georgia settlements justified him, and that the only way for the United States to be respected by foreign powers was by defending its own territory. The raids that the Spanish government did nothing to stop (or, perhaps encouraged) were destroying the lives and livelihoods of innocent people.

John Quincy's persuasive skills, in both speech and writing, struck a chord with President Monroe. He switched sides on the issue. It was a smart political move. The American people adamantly supported Andrew Jackson. In their eyes, he was a war hero.

As thanks, President Monroe made Jackson the first governor of Florida.

John Quincy's reasoning didn't just win over Americans. With the same genius he'd used to convince the Senate to make the Louisiana Purchase, he convinced Spanish and British officials that Jackson was innocent of wrongdoing. He argued that Spain was accountable for the actions of the people living in its territory and that, if anyone was to blame, it was the Spanish government for letting the raids happen. It was a simple argument, but his skill in presenting it was overwhelming.

One issue remained: Florida. The United States had taken over most of the territory, and the Spanish government wanted it back.

John Quincy had a solution. He led negotiations with Spain to acquire the entire territory of Florida. The treaty, now known as the Adams-Onís Treaty, was signed on February 2, 1819. In addition to the purchase of Florida, the treaty established a boundary between the United States and Spanish-owned territory in the west. The United States' western border was set along the Sabine, Red, and Arkansas rivers.

Perhaps the most brilliant part of the purchase of Florida was that it wasn't even really a purchase. Instead of payment, the United States granted Spain a highly favorable trading arrangement and paid the legal claims that Americans had made against the Spanish government, a sum of approximately $5.8 million. This was actually a tiny sum of money considering what was being acquired.

The Adams-Onís Treaty was another massive accomplishment by John Quincy.

But he wasn't happy. He was devastated.

Loss

On August 28, 1818, Abigail Adams had passed away. She was 73 years old. John Quincy's heart overflowed with grief. He emptied it into his diary.

"Never have I known another human being the perpetual object of whose life was… to do good. It was a necessity of her nature… there is no virtue in the female heart that was not the ornament of hers" (Adams).

Abigail's death rattled the foundation of her son's psyche to its core, but he didn't let that stop him. He kept working.

After the treaty was signed, he threw himself into his next task: being an Adams.

It wasn't easy. Finances, three under-achieving children, an alcoholic brother, and an elderly father were all pressing concerns. The stress was worsened the fact that drama in his personal life could harm his public image.

The warm, relaxed John Quincy from England was gone for good. Now in his place was an aggressively dedicated perfectionist.

He still read constantly. Alexander Pope and the Bible were two favorite sources of comfort. His massive knowledge of literature served him well. As he entertained ideas of being President of the United States, he achieved the title in two other organizations. He became President of the American Bible Society and the American Academy of Arts and Sciences.

Neither office took up much of his time. This was lucky. In Washington, a divisive issue was finally coming into the public spotlight.

That issue was slavery.

John Quincy had first been exposed to slavery in Berlin when he was only a child. It had disgusted him. As an adult, his feelings hadn't changed. But his thoughts had certainly evolved. As a child, he regarded slavery as bad. As an adult, he regarded it more as a moral, political, and religious issue. He saw slavery as morally corrupt, politically divisive, and religiously offensive.

A woodcut from 1837 that accompanied the anti-slavery poem "Our Countrymen in Chains" by John Greenleaf Whittier.[2]

"It is among the evils of slavery that it taints the very sources of moral principle. It establishes false estimates of virtue and vice; for what can be more false and heartless than this doctrine which makes the first and holiest rights of humanity to depend upon the color of the skin? …It perverts human reason… to maintain that slavery is sanctioned by the Christian religion, that slaves are happy are contented in their condition, that between master and slave there are tie of mutual attachment and affection, that the virtues of the master are refined and exalted by the degradation of the slave… The bargain between freedom and slavery contained in the Constitution of the United States is morally and politically vicious, inconsistent with the principles upon which alone our Revolution can be justified" (Adams).

This rant is from a diary entry by John Quincy, but he didn't limit his thoughts on slavery to just his diary. He would spend the rest of his life making them known.

Many politicians were slave-owners, including President Monroe himself.

The issue split Washington right down the middle. In the middle was President Monroe who, despite being a slave-owner, didn't appear to have a strong opinion on the issue either way. In fact, he tried to avoid involving himself in it as much as possible.

In 1819, slavery was legal in 11 states and illegal in 11 others. The issue was splitting the country in half as well. But, at the time, there wasn't much John Quincy could do about it.

Henry Clay publicly opposed slavery despite owning slaves himself. Seeing that the United States was headed toward civil war, he drafted a plan to preserve peace. That plan would come to be known as the Missouri Compromise.

At the time, a big part of the slavery debate was how slavery should be handled in the western territories. Southerners wanted it to be legal, while northerners wanted it to be banned.

Henry Clay's idea was simple: in the northern part of the territories (except for Missouri) slavery would be outlawed. In the southern part of the territories, slavery would be permitted. It was a disappointment to both sides, but they were tired of fighting and a flawed solution seemed better than no solution at all.

At the time, Missouri was in the process of being admitted to the U.S. as a state. There was political controversy over the fact that, as a state, Missouri would be able to send representatives to Washington who'd support slavery. To maintain the balance of power between free states and slave states, Maine was admitted as a free state as part of the compromise.

John Quincy supported the Missouri Compromise. Like Clay, he believed that preventing civil war was the most pressing concern. He recognized that a civil war could only end in massive bloodshed, and that bloodshed would leave the United States weakened and vulnerable to attacks from foreign powers.

The compromise worked — at least for the time being. It doused the flames of animosity between the north and south, but embers of tension were still there, burning beneath the surface.

Minor Midlife Crisis

The issue of slavery, while far from resolved, no longer had the United States on the brink of war. This allowed John Quincy to apply his energy and talents on a new project.

The project was himself.

His life had passed the half-century mark and middle age had not greeted him warmly. Despite the importance of his duties, or perhaps because of it, he began to have difficulty focusing on his work. The endless avalanche of paperwork that found its way to his desk caused him constant annoyance. So did the endless series of balls, banquets, and meetings that found their way onto his calendar.

People and paperwork weren't exactly his favorite companions. He preferred the company of a good book and often found himself reading Cicero and the Bible at the expense of his official duties.

To make up for wasted time, and to feed his overwhelming hunger to be productive, he began staying up late into the night, often getting no more than four hours of sleep.

This attempt to increase his productivity turned out to be counter-productive. He found himself exhausted all hours of the day. His temper, while never violent or cruel, became sour and unpleasant.

John Quincy, always introspective, was aware of all of this. He wasn't happy with any of it.

His diary entries were peppered with bits of self-criticism and promises to do better. He blamed his lack of productivity on his inability to focus and his love of food and wine, which left him feeling sluggish in the evening hours.

But his attempts at self-growth were hampered by more family-related stress.

Tom, his brother, was slipping further and further into the depths of despair. Alcoholism and gambling had tightened their crushing grip on his life. His legal practice was failing and his properties weren't being managed. He also had more debts and children than he knew what to do with.

John Quincy, upon seeing his brother during a brief vacation to Quincy, promised to help.

He agreed to support Tom's family financially. He also bought several pieces of property from him, which was also an act of charity, considering their state of neglect.

Tom promised to get sober. It was a promise he had broken before, and one he would break again.

After returning to Washington D.C., John Quincy found that his focus hadn't improved. The joys of his favorite pastimes, such as reading works of philosophy, writing in his journal, and bathing in the Potomac River, became tinged with guilt.

By most standards, he was being too hard on himself. He was doing his job and doing it well. But the standard of perfectionism that he held himself to was seared into his mind and he couldn't control it.

However, he could use it to his advantage. His overachieving mindset and painstaking attention to detail served him well in yet another project.

With his guidance, a report on systems of weights and measurements was being crafted for Congress. This was important. The country needed one standard for measuring height, width, depth, distance, volume, etc. Up until that time, several standards were used throughout the country, which often led to confusion.

John Quincy obsessed over the project, which consumed massive amounts of his time. The rest of the year 1820 flew by in a barrage of research and writing.

It wasn't until February 22, 1821, that John Quincy presented the *Report of the Secretary of State Upon Weights and Measures* to Congress.

Three months earlier, the 1820 Presidential Election ended with James Monroe being reelected. Since the Federalist Party was on its last leg, it hadn't even nominated a candidate to run against him.

John Quincy knew that things were only going to get harder. "As the first term… has hitherto been the period of the greatest national tranquility… it appears to me scarcely avoidable that the second term will be among the most stormy and violent" (Adams).

John Quincy's Speech

A re-election for James Monroe meant a re-election for John Quincy. Considering what he'd accomplished in his four years as secretary of state, he may have doubted that the next four would be as productive.

By the summer of 1821, it wasn't looking like they would be. John Quincy found himself bored and underwhelmed with his life. He complained of wanting "…an object of pursuit which may engage my feelings and excite constant interest, leaving as few hours as possible for listlessness."

Not that he had many hours reserved for listlessness. Spanish and Russian territorial claims to land on the North American continent were a cause for concern. As head of the State Department, John Quincy found himself increasingly irritated by foreign powers involving themselves in American affairs. He wanted to put a stop to it.

On Independence Day, after a reading of the Declaration of Independence, John Quincy delivered an oration that would echo through the pages of history.

"…There was a single plain and almost self-evident principle–that man has a right to the exercise of his own reason… The triumph of reason was the result of inquiry and discussion. Centuries of desolating wars have succeeded, and oceans of human blood have flowed, for the final establishment of this principle; but it was from the darkness… that the first spark was emitted, and from the arches of a university that it first kindled into day… Thus was a social compact formed upon the elementary principles of civil society, in which conquest and servitude had no part. The slough of brutal force was entirely cast off; all was voluntary; all was unbiased consent; all was the agreement of soul with soul" (Adams).

He went on to say that, "…America, with the same voice which spoke herself into existence as a nation, proclaimed to mankind the inextinguishable rights of human nature, and the only lawful foundations of government… She has uniformly spoken… the language of equal liberty, equal justice, and equal rights."

The speech, as powerful as it was by itself, was only a prelude to something much bigger. And it's incredibly fitting that it came after a reading of the Declaration of Independence.

John Quincy's philosophy of American independence was going to inspire one of the most important documents in the nation's history.

The Monroe Doctrine

Two years passed. On the surface, they seemed uneventful. John Quincy kept busy meeting foreign officials, discussing trade deals, keeping his journal, and trying to bring order to his chaotic family.

But there was more to it than that. In December of 1823, James Monroe delivered a speech to Congress. The speech, which was only 956 words long, would become known as the Monroe Doctrine.

A more appropriate name would have been the John Quincy Adams Doctrine. John Quincy not only wrote it, he convinced James Monroe to accept the philosophy behind it.

"Our policy, in regard to Europe, which was adopted at an early stage of the wars which have so long agitated that quarter of the globe, nevertheless remains the same, which is, not to interfere in the internal concerns of any of its powers... and to preserve those relations by a frank, firm, and manly policy; meeting, in all instances, the just claims of every power; submitting to injuries from none" (Renehan).

In his famously verbose style, John Quincy had sent a warning to the rest of the world. And most importantly, a warning to Spain.

The most critical foreign policy concern the U.S. had in 1823 was Spain. The Spanish were losing control of their previously massive empire in the new world. Spain planned to send armies to Mexico and Central America to squash the new republics that had sprouted up.

John Quincy didn't think Spain would have been content with getting back the territories it had recently lost. He recognized the possibility that Spain would become greedy and try to expand. He also recognized that Latin Americans had a right to claim independence. Freedom from foreign rule was an idea that the United States was founded on. Therefore, the Monroe Doctrine made it clear that European interference in the new world would be regarded as hostile.

The Monroe Doctrine would later be referenced by many future presidents, including Grant, Teddy Roosevelt, Franklin Delano Roosevelt, and Kennedy.

But it wouldn't take that long to become relevant. The Monroe Doctrine immediately created political tidal waves. The United States had suffered from European harassment throughout its half-century of existence. England, France, and Spain had viewed the new world as a prize to be won and a territory to be conquered. Finally, that chapter in American history was over.

And John Quincy Adams had written the final word.

Sources

1   Photo Credit: Everett – Art / Shutterstock.com

2   Photo Credit: Everett Historical / Shutterstock.com

Chapter 14: Adams for President

Election Season

The political landscape had changed a lot in the last four years. The Federalist Party had collapsed, leaving the Democratic-Republican Party as the only major party in the country. The requirement that voters must own land had been repealed, greatly expanding the voter base. Also, James Monroe did not intend to run for a third term in office. He'd run unopposed in 1820.

1824, however, wasn't going to be a one-man race. As expected, Henry Clay decided to run. So did Secretary of the Treasury William H. Crawford. Also entering the race was Senator Andrew Jackson, and he was riding a huge wave of support. Voters respected him for his service in the War of 1812 and the First Seminole War.

Secretary of War John C. Calhoun also made a bid for the White House. However, he saw that he had little support and dropped out, setting his sights instead on vice presidency, an office he would ultimately win. Smith Thompson also entered the race, but dropped out when he received almost no support, like Calhoun.

Another man entered the race too. John Quincy Adams, to the delight of his friends and family members, decided to campaign for the presidency.

A FOOT-RACE

Etching by David Claypoole Johnston portraying the 1824 election. From left to right, candidates John Quincy Adams, William Crawford, and Andrew Jackson can be seen running toward the finish line. Cheering citizens can be seen in the background.[1]

It wasn't an easy decision for him. He was a proud man, and the possibility of utter failure terrified him. But, to his delight, he found himself popular. Thanks to his roles in the Louisiana Purchase, the Treaty of Ghent, the Adams-Onís Treaty, and the Monroe Doctrine, he'd put together quite a résumé.

But he wasn't without faults. His messy appearance, which Abigail had often criticized, came across as off-putting and even led to him being mocked by a newspaper.

Another issue was his formal style of communication. It made him respected by other intellectuals, but, to the average person, someone who churned out so many long-winded sentences peppered with references to classical literature could be hard to understand. And who would vote for someone they can't understand?

John Quincy was aware of these problems, but, true to his stubborn nature, did little about them. However, there was another problem — one he would do something about.

A smear campaign masterminded by Henry Clay was threatening to discredit John Quincy.

Clay's ally, Jonathan Russell, had served alongside Clay and John Quincy as a negotiator to help produce the Treaty of Ghent. He began spreading the lie that John Quincy had offered to give the British rights to the Mississippi River.

Russell's lie, if believed, would have ruined John Quincy's chances with voters living along or near the Mississippi River.

But John Quincy, being the meticulous record-keeper that he was, produced documents from the negotiations in Ghent proving that Russell's claims were false.

As a result, Henry Clay's campaign was damaged and Russell's career in Washington was destroyed. John Quincy refuted him so effectively that the name "Jonathan Russell" became a verb — to Jonathan Russell someone is to beat them so badly in an argument that their credibility is ruined.

The attack on John Quincy's character and career hadn't just given him the opportunity to execute a counter-attack. In addition to making Clay look foolish for his association with Russell, the massively detailed rebuttal composed by John Quincy made him look like the kind of serious, detail-oriented, hard-working man that most voters wanted.

But, aside from the Jonathan Russell controversy, John Quincy's campaign was minimalistic. As his opponents constantly attacked him and each other, John Quincy stayed mostly quiet. He considered himself, and the presidency, to be above all the mudslinging.

A bizarre moment came when John Quincy, to the utter surprise of everyone, including his own wife, announced his intention to host a celebration in Andrew Jackson's honor. The celebration was for the ninth anniversary of Jackson's victory over the British in the Battle of New Orleans. Hundreds of guests poured into the Adams home, waiting to see if one man would attack the other, or if the two would officially join forces.

Neither happened. John Quincy and Andrew Jackson spoke highly of one another. Even though Jackson would refuse John Quincy's offer to run as his vice president, the celebration itself went smoothly.

It was a strange move. Despite his intention to run for the presidency, John Quincy didn't seem too interested in promoting himself as the top person for the job.

His reservations were probably nothing more than a clumsy attempt at mental gymnastics. If he didn't try so hard to win the presidency, maybe he wouldn't feel as bad if he ended up losing it.

But, fortunately for John Quincy, he didn't have to campaign much. At least, not directly. His body of work was campaigning for him.

The Monroe Doctrine had reshaped American culture. Without the constant fear of foreign invasion, Americans were free to focus on building. Building roads, railroads, bridges, canals, and towns. The United States was on its way to becoming a world power. And it owed a great deal of that newfound power to John Quincy Adams.

Going into the election season, Henry Clay had been the obvious threat to John Quincy. And yes, Clay's ruthless ambition and hunger for the presidency made him a powerful opponent. But John Quincy's strongest challenge was Andrew Jackson.

Jackson's record as a war hero made him legendary among Americans. And, regardless of how significant John Quincy's achievements were, the battles he'd won with his pen just didn't seem as impressive as the battles Jackson had won with his sword.

Meanwhile, John Quincy's oldest son, George Washington Adams, graduated from Harvard and his youngest son, Charles Francis, enrolled in Harvard. His middle son, John Adams II, was already enrolled in Harvard. All three of their academic records were painfully average. "I had hoped that at least one of my sons would have been ambitious to excel. I find them all three coming to manhood with indolent minds," wrote John Quincy.

John Quincy wasn't shy about making his feelings known to his sons. Unfortunately, his tough love style of parenting backfired. John Adams II was expelled from Harvard for participating in a riot, and, in disgrace, returned home to his parents.

To the wannabe president's luck, this was an age before social media. Most people didn't know or care about his rigid parenting style or his children's failure to "excel."

As the campaigning process continued, John Quincy turned, once again, to his journal to confide his feelings about himself and his role in the world. "I have followed the convictions of my own mind with a single eye to the interests of the whole nation," he wrote. He also wrote that, "The bitterness and violence of Presidential electioneering increase as the time advances. The uncertainty of the event continues as great as ever. It seems as if every great liar... was at work day and night to destroy my character" (Adams).

As Election Day drew near, John Quincy worried that all the mudslinging would stain his image forever. To his surprise and delight, it didn't. The old saying (which, in 1824, hadn't even been said yet) that, "whatever doesn't kill you only makes you stronger" seemed to apply to John Quincy's campaign.

Fast Fact: James Monroe believed that John Quincy was the most qualified and best-fitting man for the job. However, he kept his thoughts private, believing it to be beyond his role as the sitting president to comment on the upcoming election.

A Stalemate

It was finally happening. It was December, and the 1824 election was finally happening.

Votes were being cast and the candidates were waiting with bated breath for the winner to be announced.

Only, there was no winner. Once the votes were tallied, it was clear that none of the four men had earned a majority of the votes. The Constitution required that, to be voted into office, a single candidate needed more votes than every other candidate combined. Just having more votes than any other single candidate wasn't enough.

For the first time in American history, the battle for the White House had ended in a draw. So who would become president? According to the Constitution, that was for the House of Representatives to decide.

The fact that he hadn't won infuriated Andrew Jackson. With over 150,000 votes, he'd received more support than any other candidate. (John Quincy came in second with about 114,000). In his mind, that meant that he deserved the office.

His supporters agreed. Vocally.

The House of Representatives was scheduled to meet on February 9, 1825, to decide who would become the nation's sixth president.

Candidates used this window of time to convince as many congressmen as they could to support them.

Clay had an advantage. As Speaker of the House, he was in a unique position to influence the outcome of the election. To the surprise of no one, he used it. To the surprise of everyone, he didn't use it for himself.

Henry Clay despised Andrew Jackson. He despised him so much that, on January 9, he informed John Quincy that he intended to publicly support him.

John Quincy had mixed feelings about the whole situation. Winning the presidency despite losing the popular vote would, he feared, be a hollow victory.

As promised, Henry Clay threw his support behind John Quincy.

On February 9, the House of Representatives made its decision. Later that day, John Quincy received the news.

President-elect John Quincy, that is, received the news.

The Corrupt Bargain

John Quincy was elated, but he still harbored doubts about being president. The weight of the responsibility threatened to crush his sanity.

And maybe it did, because John Quincy made an insane mistake. He and Henry Clay, despite their history, saw eye-to-eye on a lot of issues. They both believed in a strong federal government. A federal government that oversaw expansion. A federal government that funded public works projects like roads, bridges, and dams. (Andrew Jackson didn't agree with any of that. That's why Henry Clay had supported John Quincy.)

Deciding to forgive Clay for his past attempts to sabotage him, John Quincy offered Clay the position of Secretary of State. Clay accepted.

Just like that, John Quincy's presidency was off to a terrible start. And it hadn't even started yet.

As soon as Clay's appointment was announced, Andrew Jackson and his supporters exploded with rage.

John Quincy and Henry Clay were accused of a "corrupt bargain." They were accused of conspiring to cheat Andrew Jackson out of his rightful place in history. John Quincy had, according to Jackson and his supporters, given Clay his appointment in exchange for Clay's support.

They accused the president-elect of buying his way into office. It was a serious charge and it stuck.

To this day, it's not known for sure if Jackson's accusations are true or not. But, they were so convincing that even John Quincy's supporters were angry with him.

On Friday, March 4, 1825, John Quincy Adams put his hand on a book of constitutional law and took his oath of office. He then gave his first speech as President John Quincy Adams.

"In compliance with an usage coeval with the existence of our Federal Constitution, and sanctioned by the example of my predecessors in the career upon which I am about to enter, I appear, my fellow-citizens, in your presence and in that of Heaven to bind myself by the solemnities of religious obligation to the faithful performance of the duties allotted to me in the station to which I have been called" (Dickins).

So far, so good. The crowd was mostly on John Quincy's side. But then he lost them.

"The roads and aqueducts of Rome have been the admiration of all after ages, and have survived thousands of years after all her conquests have been swallowed up in despotism or become the spoil of barbarians. Some diversity of opinion has prevailed with regard to the powers of Congress for legislation upon objects of this nature... But nearly twenty years have passed since the construction of the first national road was commenced. The authority for its construction was then unquestioned. To how many thousands of our countrymen has it proved a benefit? To what single individual has it ever proved an injury? Repeated, liberal, and candid discussions in the Legislature have conciliated the sentiments and approximated the opinions of enlightened minds upon the question of constitutional power. I can not but hope that by the same process of friendly, patient, and persevering deliberation all constitutional objections will ultimately be removed. The extent and limitation of the powers of the General Government in relation to this transcendently important interest will be settled and acknowledged to the common satisfaction of all, and every speculative scruple will be solved by a practical public blessing" (Dickins).

Long-winded paragraphs like that annoyed the crowd. No one likes being spoken down to, and bizarre references to ancient Roman culture did nothing to make John Quincy seem more accessible. Or likeable.

By the end of his speech, which actually ended up being pretty short, despite its density, John Quincy hadn't succeeded in getting his message across to his audience. In fact, he'd only succeeded in annoying them.

It was a cold, rainy day — the kind that makes everything seem bleak. And things were going to seem bleak for a long time.

Within the first few minutes of his presidency, John Quincy had set the mood for the four years that would follow.

Sources

1   Photo Credit: Library of Congress / Created by: Boston : Crackfardi Delt. et Sct. David Claypool Johnston / Call Number: PC/US - 1824.J635, no. 1 (A size) [P&P]

Chapter 15: President Adams

Recluse-in-Chief

Sadly, for John Quincy, the events that happened right before he took office ended up being a lot more exciting than most of what happened when he was actually in office.

His image had been destroyed by the "corrupt bargain" and, to be an effective president, he needed to repair it. That would mean giving speeches, hosting parties, and getting out of the White House enough to cultivate a real presence in Washington.

John Quincy didn't do any of that. In fact, his seclusion became more severe than ever.

His was seen as an arrogant intellectual who had no concern for or understanding of the average American. His opponents had painted him that way, and he sat still, letting the paint dry.

A portrait of John Quincy Adams.[1]

Being associated with him became political poison. His former friends and colleagues in Washington avoided him. They saw his unpopularity as a disease and feared he was contagious.

John Quincy was politically crippled.

His ideas were brilliant, though. He wanted to send the United States to the center of the global stage. His plan to build on and expand the nation's infrastructure would cultivate the western states from a backwoods abyss into an economic powerhouse.

"Roads and canals, by multiplying and facilitating the communications and intercourse between distant regions and multitudes of men, are among the most important means of improvement" (Koch).

Of course, his economic vision would eventually come to pass — long after he was out of office, and precious years of potential progress were lost.

John Quincy spent his days sulking around the White House. Before taking office, he'd been afraid of the presidency. He'd been worried that he wouldn't be able to handle it.

There was nothing to handle. Except boredom.

As a political leper, John Quincy found himself with little to do and a massive amount of time with which to do it.

John Quincy finally got some relief from his routine when Marquis De Lafayette visited the White House. The two first met when John Quincy was living in Paris at age 15 and they had remained friends.

A banquet was held at the White House in celebration of Lafayette's 68th birthday. John Quincy gave a touching speech at the party. He praised Lafayette's heroism in the Revolutionary War and thanked him on behalf of the United States.

Before leaving to return to France, Lafayette gave John Quincy a gift. And not an ordinary gift, like a book or a bottle of wine. He gave John Quincy a pet alligator. John Quincy accepted. He kept his new pet in the unfinished east wing of the White House, where he used it to terrify guests.

Another break from the monotony of his daily routine came when he was in a boat on the Potomac River. John Quincy often swam in the river for exercise. That day, he and his assistant got a little more exercise than they wanted.

"I attempted to cross the river with Antoine in a small canoe, with a view to swim across it to come back... Before we had got half across the river, the boat had leaked itself half full, and then we found there was nothing on board to scoop up the water and throw it over. Just at that critical moment a fresh breeze from the northwest blew down the river as from the nose of a bellows. In five minutes' time it made a little tempest, and set the boat to dancing till the river came in at the sides. I jumped overboard, and Antoine did the same, and lost hold of the boat,

which filled with water and drifted away. We were as near as possible to the middle of the river, and swam to the opposite shore. Antoine, who was naked, reached it with little difficulty. I had much more, and, while struggling for life and gasping for breath, had ample leisure to reflect upon my own indiscretion... After reaching the shore, I took off my shirt and pantaloons, wrung them out, and gave them to Antoine to go and look out for our clothes, or for a person to send to the house for others, and for the carriage to come and fetch me" (Adams).

While John Quincy was playing with his new pet alligator and trying not to drown, Andrew Jackson was hard at work. He created a new political group called the Democratic Party. With it, he had a new base of political operations. He'd spend the next few years using it to constantly impede, annoy, and attack John Quincy.

The constant barrage of negative attention wasn't fun. But the pain it caused John Quincy was nothing compared to what he was about to go through.

Tragedy

John Adams hadn't been well in a long time, especially since Abigail passed away. On Independence Day of 1826, his frail health finally gave way. John Adams died at age 90.

A devastated John Quincy learned of his father's death too late to make it to the funeral. However, memorials for John Adams were held around the country and John Quincy attended several of them.

Fast Fact: Thomas Jefferson died the same day as John Adams. The U.S. was shocked to have lost two monumental figures within the span of only a few hours, especially on the nation's 50th birthday.

John Adams had left behind a will that was to benefit several people and public institutions. John Quincy was named as the trustee in charge of seeing that every detail of the will was handled properly. It was a frustrating task, as Adams' estate was a mess. In fact, over the next few months, it took up more of John Quincy's time than the presidency.

Meanwhile, John Quincy's level of support continued to decline. Midterm elections were held and most of his few remaining supporters in Congress were voted out of office.

His outlook on his political life was bleak. He made that clear in his diary, writing, "… I must wait my allotted time. My own career is closed. My hopes such as are left me are centered upon my children. George's state is precarious; and his prospects are doubtful" (Adams).

(John Quincy's concerns about George were understandable. He and John Adams II weren't doing well. Their love affair with liquor was becoming more passionate. It would become an increasingly severe problem for them.)

The president's life was reduced to reading, writing in his diary, doing what little official work he had to do, and horseback riding.

"I rise generally before five; frequently before four. Write from one to two hours in this diary. Ride about 12 miles in two hours on horseback with my son John. Return home about nine. Breakfast. And from that time till dinner, between five and six, afternoon, I am occupied incessantly with visitors, business, reading letters, dispatchers, and newspapers. I spent an hour, sometimes before and sometimes after dinner, in the garden and nursery—an hour of drowsiness on a sofa, and two hours of writing in the evening. Retire usually between 11 and midnight. My riding on horseback is a dangerous and desperate resort for the recovery of my health" (Adams).

John Quincy lived by this routine for most of his presidency. It was punctuated by the occasional public speech. Despite his gifts as a speaker, the speeches did little to help his image. He came across as boring and out of touch. Most Americans didn't care about their president's projects. Improving infrastructure and increasing educational funding didn't appeal to a nation of farmers, ranchers, and tradesmen.

Stress had taken its toll on John Quincy's health. He endured countless stomachaches that ruined his appetite and searing headaches left him miserable for hours on end.

Fast Fact: Abigail Adams had suffered from severe migraines. Many suspect that they were triggered by family-related stress.

Just when the well of John Quincy's suffering seemed like it would never go dry, something surprised him.

It was 1828. John Quincy's term in office was coming to a close. As a matter of pride, he planned to seek reelection, but he had no delusions about his political situation. He didn't expect to win. In fact, he didn't expect to receive any support.

That expectation was shattered by the voices of thousands of people in Philadelphia. John Quincy was returning to Washington from a fishing trip. When his boat stopped in the city, countless well-wishers poured out of the woodwork to greet their president. The crowd gave him three massive cheers, a gesture that stunned John Quincy. He shook hundreds of hands before departing.

The show of support restored some of John Quincy's faith in himself. But it was too little and it came far too late.

The 1828 election was around the corner and Andrew Jackson, true to his military background, had rallied his army.

Sources
1   Photo Credit: Oleg Golovnev / Shutterstock.com

Chapter 16: The 1828 Election

Fierce Opposition

Ideally, a presidential race would be a lively exchange of ideas, a battleground of minds. But the 1828 U.S. Presidential Election wasn't ideal. At least, it wasn't ideal for John Quincy. It was shaping up to be a battleground of mindlessness. Instead of ideas, the candidates exchanged insults.

Well, sort of. John Quincy considered himself above that style of rhetoric. However, his supporters didn't.

And their favorite target was Andrew Jackson's wife. Rachel Jackson was married to another man before she met Andrew. Her first husband had been cruel and abusive and she'd left him. However, they weren't actually divorced when Jackson married her. That made her marriage to Jackson legally invalid.

One newspaper, the Cincinnati Gazette, published an article asking, "Ought a convicted adulteress and her paramour husband be placed in the highest offices of this free and Christian land?" (Remini).

Jackson was enraged and his wife was mortified. Understandably so. Rachel *was* divorced from her first husband. The divorce simply hadn't been finalized when she remarried. She was being brutally attacked based on nothing more than a technicality.

Jackson's opponents didn't stop there. They wrote articles describing him as a mindless, ill-tempered, aggressive lunatic. They also took to referring to him as "jackass," which would go on to inspire the use of the donkey as the symbol for the Democratic Party.

Jackson wasn't about to turn the other cheek. He and his supporters amplified their attacks on John Quincy. They falsely accused him of giving an American servant girl to Russian Czar Alexander I to do with as he pleased.

On a more petty note, they accused him of wasting public funds on what they referred to as gambling devices. The devices turned out to be a pool table and a chess set. Hardly a financial scandal, especially since John Quincy's careful budgeting as president had resulted in the public debt dropping from over $16 million to under $5 million.

Other members of John Quincy's cabinet were attacked too. Henry Clay was so upset by the negative press that he took a sabbatical for the sake of his health.

The Sting of Defeat

On October 31, the voting began. Results were announced on December 3. To the surprise of few and the joy of many, Andrew Jackson won in a landslide with over 640,000 votes and 178 electoral votes. John Quincy received a little over 500,000 votes and only 83 electoral votes.

FIRST CAPITOL INAUGURATION · 1829

President Andrew Jackson being sworn in by Chief Justice John Marshall at the U.S. Capitol on March 4, 1829.[1]

Both men were bitter. John Quincy was bitter because he'd lost and Jackson was bitter because, just three weeks after it was announced that he'd won the election, his wife passed away. The humiliation and stress she'd endured during the campaign was believed to have contributed to her poor health, which had grown progressively worse during her last few months alive.

Jackson considered John Quincy partly to blame for his wife's death, despite the fact that he had nothing to do with the attacks on her.

He stayed bitter for the rest of his life.

John Quincy didn't attend Jackson's inauguration. He and Louisa packed their things and prepared to leave Washington D.C. They planned to return to Quincy and hoped that, after four years of misery, they could finally enjoy their lives.

They couldn't.

John Quincy's worst fear came true. He and Louisa received news that George Washington Adams, their firstborn son, had died. He was only 28 years old.

His death came after he'd gotten drunk and fallen off of a steamboat. It was impossible to know if his death had been an accident or a suicide.

John Quincy and Louisa were devastated. It was especially hard on Louisa. She'd endured so many miscarriages. Losing her firstborn son was more than she could handle. It sucked the marrow out of her soul.

She stayed in Washington D.C., deciding that she wasn't up to traveling.

John Quincy bought her a home on a small plot of land and went to Quincy. "The parting of my wife was distressing to her and to me… We parted with anguish I cannot describe."

Sources

1   Photo Credit: Everett Historical / Shutterstock.com

Part 4: Before I Retire From the World

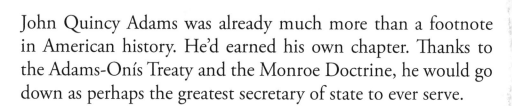

John Quincy Adams was already much more than a footnote in American history. He'd earned his own chapter. Thanks to the Adams-Onís Treaty and the Monroe Doctrine, he would go down as perhaps the greatest secretary of state to ever serve.

His presidency had mostly been a disappointment. However, despite not accomplishing what he'd set out to accomplish, he could still brag that he'd eliminated most of the national debt. And, during his time in office, the U.S. was not involved in any foreign conflicts.

After leaving office, he decided to retire. He told his friends, family, and colleagues that he was finished. But he wasn't finished.

Far from it.

The debate on slavery was returning to public consciousness. John Quincy had always hated slavery but hadn't been able to do much about it. That was finally about to change.

Chapter 17: Adams for Congress

Back to Washington

John Quincy spent his time writing, planting trees, going for walks, and organizing his father's papers. It was a simple life. But not a fulfilling one.

To the surprise of perhaps no one but himself, he found himself wanting more. The urge to serve his country returned. He tried to ignore the urge, hoping it would go away.

But it only kept growing.

Still, it wasn't enough to want to return to work. He needed to hold an office. That meant running in an election. He just didn't feel ready for that. Not yet.

On September 17, 1829, he attended a celebration in Boston. It was the 200th anniversary of the city's founding, and the people there greeted John Quincy warmly.

By feeling welcome, he was massively overjoyed. During the festivities, he was taken aside by Congressman Reverend Joseph Richardson and a few of his friends. He told John Quincy that he had something important to discuss with him. They agreed to meet the following day.

Richardson was planning to retire. He wanted someone with brilliance and a backbone to take over his office for him. He wanted John Quincy to run for Congress.

John Quincy promised to think it over. Losing meant being humiliated again. But the Congressional district was centered in Quincy and he figured he had a pretty good shot at winning.

He decided to take it.

Louisa wasn't happy. She'd only escaped the White House a few months earlier. The idea of John Quincy putting himself, and her, through the stress of running for and serving in a public office again was overwhelming.

John Quincy didn't listen. He decided to run for the Congressional seat.

He won easily, receiving more than triple the votes of the other two candidates combined (1817 to 552). Despite winning the office in November of 1830, he wouldn't be able to take office until the 22nd Congress convened over a year later.

Staying true to his nature, John Quincy kicked off his return to politics with a controversial speech while still in Quincy. The speech blasted "nullification," a concept popular in the southern states that asserted states had the right to override any federal law except Constitutional provisions.

John Quincy argued that nullification was, "nothing less than treason." His oration was hugely popular and copies of it were published across the nation, both in newspapers and as pamphlets. John Quincy had accomplished something significant even before having officially taken his new office.

The very day he delivered this oration, James Monroe died, making him the third president to die on July 4 (after John Adams and Thomas Jefferson). John Quincy gave a heartfelt (and politically charged) eulogy of his former leader, emphasizing the need for a federal government that has authority over its states. The eulogy was also widely published.

John Quincy had an abundance of time on his hands before he was to take office. He used it to relax and write poetry.

Finally, he and Louisa left for Washington D.C. in December of 1830. On March 4, 1831, he took office.

Rebel With a Cause

When he took office, John Quincy made abolishing slavery his number one priority. It wasn't going to be easy. In Congress, the anti-slavery movement was just a whisper compared to the chorus of shouts that was the pro-slavery movement. Even though almost every northern Congressman was opposed to slavery, they were shy about it. The possibility of southern states seceding from the U.S. terrified many of them. The anti-slavery cause needed a voice. And no one was as vocal about slavery as John Quincy.

But not at first. When he first got elected to Congress, John Quincy's focus wasn't on slavery. He was too busy with his committee.

Congressional committees were groups of congressmen who handled specific duties. To his annoyance, John Quincy was appointed chairman of the Committee on Manufacturers.

As chairman, he was drawn into debates on banking and tariffs. He accomplished little in this role and began to regret returning to politics.

On March 13, 1832, John Quincy's only remaining sibling passed away. Tom was deeply in debt when he died of alcoholism, leaving a financial mess for John Quincy to sort out.

It was a hard blow for John Quincy, but, having already lost both parents, two children, and four siblings, he had learned to deal with grief.

At least, he thought he had.

John Quincy kept busy writing poetry and running for governor of Massachusetts. He found success as a poet. His book, *Dermot Mac Morrogh or the Conquest of Ireland* was published in 1833. His run for governor, however, was a failure. Fellow congressman John Davis beat him easily.

Whatever misery John Quincy suffered from losing was nothing compared what he'd suffer the following year.

On October 23, 1834, John Adams II passed away after suffering from multiple seizures. He was 31. John Quincy was by his bedside when he passed away. Losing another son was mentally devastating. To John Quincy, happiness was like a priceless vase. Whenever someone he loved passed away, that vase was smashed and had to be glued back together. After being smashed so many times, it no longer seemed worth gluing together again. He and Louisa had outlived three of their children. And that's not counting the miscarriages she'd suffered through.

Alcohol had claimed another person John Quincy loved. It also claimed his peace of mind. When he returned to Congress after burying his son, he did so with renewed purpose. He decided to keep his demons at bay by staying busy.

The debate on slavery had grown stale. John Quincy breathed new life into it. He became Congress's most outspoken enemy of slavery. His opponents despised him. And they had the perfect plan to shut him up.

At least, they thought they did.

They passed what became known as the gag rule. The gag rule was a resolution that automatically tabled petitions that dealt with slavery.

The anti-slavery congressmen saw the gag rule as an unbeatable obstacle. Except John Quincy. He saw it as a challenge.

And he rose to it.

John Quincy dedicated massive amounts of time to fighting the gag rule. He found loopholes. The gag rule stated that petitions by taxpayers concerning slavery couldn't be read aloud in Congress. So John Quincy collected petitions by women, who couldn't vote at the time, and read them aloud. When confronted, he pointed out that he technically wasn't violating the gag rule.

Congress closed that loophole. John Quincy found another one. He collected and read anti-slavery prayers in Congress. When criticized, he responded that he hadn't read petitions, resolutions, or propositions. Only prayers. And Congress hadn't banned that.

John Quincy's tactics often led to loud arguments between himself and southern congressmen, especially James K. Polk, Speaker of the House.

Of course, he didn't just infuriate congressmen. Countless supporters of "slavocracy" sent angry letters to John Quincy. And the spelling and penmanship weren't the worst part of them. Many of the letters contained death threats.

John Quincy kept a clear head on his shoulders — even when his enemies threatened to cut it off.

John Quincy didn't care that people of that nature weren't on his side. He knew history itself was.

Speaking of history, John Quincy made it again when he won a Supreme Court case in 1841.

In the case, John Quincy defended the African captives of the Spanish ship the *Amistad*. The Africans had killed two of their captors and tried to force the rest to set sail back to Africa.

As the Africans were not sailors, they had no navigational skills. They didn't realize their captors had waited until nightfall and simply turned the ship toward the United States. The ship was captured by an American vessel near New York City.

John Quincy argued that the Africans were justified in their actions. After all, they'd been kidnapped from their homeland and were simply acting in self-defense.

One day, while in court, he argued for four hours *without stopping*. And the courtroom wasn't bored out of its mind. In fact, it was mesmerized.

John Quincy won. He won freedom for the Africans and he won a huge symbolic victory for the anti-slavery movement.

He made history yet again when, in 1843, he became the first U.S. president to be photographed.

By that point, he'd been in Congress for 13 years. Still, the opposing the gag rule dominated his life. He'd earned the nickname "old man eloquent" for his endless verbal confrontations with his political enemies.

On December 3, 1844, the House of Representatives called a vote on a petition regarding the gag order. John Quincy had written the petition. And, since he'd already tried this several times before, he wasn't holding his breath.

But what happened took his breath away. By a vote of 108-80, the gag order was repealed. His absurdly long struggle, his 13-year war on the gag order was finally over.

And he'd won.

John Quincy, at 78 years old, had made yet another mark on the world.

Sources
1   Photo Credit: Wikimedia Commons / Public Domain

President John Quincy Adams photographed by Philip Haas in 1843. Some historians argue that the photo was really taken in 1847, one year before Adams died.[1]

Chapter 18: End of an Era

The Lot of Mortal Men

It was November of 1846. John Quincy and Louisa were visiting Charles Francis in Boston when it happened. John Quincy suffered a massive stroke that left him unable to see or speak. A doctor informed his family that he would not recover.

But then he recovered. Not fully, but, in only a month's time, he'd regained most of his vision and speech. Walking wasn't easy, but he refused to let the handicap stop him.

He returned to Congress, determined to get back to work. When he entered the House of Representatives, he received a massive round of applause from his colleagues.

Daily life proved difficult. No longer able to walk the distance, he had to ride a horse to Congress every day, which he did without complaining.

The Mexican-American War was underway. John Quincy opposed the war and wrote two petitions to withdraw U.S. forces from Mexico.

Neither petition was accepted.

On February 3, 1848, the war ended in American victory. A petition was presented to the House to publicly give thanks to the American generals for their leadership in the war. John Quincy, disgusted by the war, shot to his feet.

"No!" he shouted.

The petition passed anyway.

Then roll was called for the next petition. John Quincy stood when his named was called. Then he collapsed. The color left his face and the light left his eyes. John Quincy was having another stroke.

He passed out. He fellow congressmen carried him to another room and placed him on a sofa.

Upon hearing news that John Quincy Adams was dying, his former enemy Henry Clay rushed to his side. He held John Quincy's hand and cried.

Louisa, of course, was devastated. She'd been married to John Quincy for over 50 years. She and Charles Francis sat by his side.

For a brief moment, John Quincy regained consciousness and managed to speak. "This is the last of earth. I am content."

John Quincy Adams lying unconscious a few hours before his death after suffering a stroke on February 23, 1848.[1]

He lay in a coma for two days.

Then, on the evening of February 23, 1848, the light of John Quincy's life, the light that illuminated eight decades of American history — finally went out.

The death of John Quincy Adams was mourned on a scale not seen since George Washington passed away.

His body was placed on a train and taken to Boston. On the way, thousands upon thousands of supporters stood by the tracks, paying their final respects.

The story of John Quincy Adams ended where it began. His body was buried in Quincy. During his funeral, soldiers stood on Penn's Hill, where John Quincy had watched the Battle of Bunker Hill unfold so many years ago.

After Reverend William Lunt delivered a heartfelt eulogy to thousands of grieving citizens, the soldiers fired their rifles in salute. The shots only echoed for an instant, but the life of John Quincy Adams would echo through American history forever.

Sources
1   Photo Credit: Everett Historical / Shutterstock.com

Conclusion

Now you know his story.

He was the first son of our second president. He spoke seven languages. He served as diplomat to four European countries. He graduated second in his class at Harvard, the college where he later became a professor. He convinced the Senate to go through with the Louisiana Purchase, which doubled the size of the United States. He led the talks with Britain that ended the War of 1812 and he negotiated the purchase of Florida from Spain.

And, in 1824, he became our sixth president. As president, he tried to push the entire country forward. But it refused to budge. He wanted better schools. His enemies didn't. He wanted more roads, canals and bridges. His enemies didn't. And he hated slavery. His enemies didn't. They stopped his policies, but they couldn't stop his ideas. John Quincy Adams was ahead of his time, and future leaders carried on his vision for America.

After losing the presidency to Andrew Jackson, he came back to politics as a congressman. He spent his nine terms in office fighting slavery. Then, at 80 years old, the man who claimed that, "The world will retire from me before I retire from the world," had his second stroke. He died in Congress, having spent his last waking moments fighting for his beliefs.

Who was John Quincy Adams? A strong-willed but kindhearted man; one of both action and understanding.

And it's important that we understand him.

The burial vault and tomb of John Quincy Adams and his wife Louisa Catherine.[1]

Sources

1   Photo Credit: Joseph Sohm / Shutterstock.com

Author's Note

John Quincy Adams is my favorite president and has been for a long time. Every once in a great while, someone will make the mistake of asking me who my favorite president is. Most people answer that question with one word (Usually "Lincoln" or "Washington").

But I can't, and not just because there were two presidents named Adams.

I always end up having to explain who he was and why I think so much of him. His presidency wasn't a big success. But his life was an enormous one.

A lot of you read this book as research for an essay or to prepare for a quiz. That's awesome. I hope you get an A+! I'm rooting for you!

But, to the dozen or so of you who actually read this *entire* book, not just what you needed for research, you deserve a special thank you. You suffered through 30,000 words of me gushing about my favorite president, and for that, you have my undying gratitude.

And to those of you bothering to read the author's note, you really are the best. (All three of you!)

But the deepest thanks, the kind that comes from the innermost chamber of the heart, is reserved for two people. Carol Lallier, the smartest person I know. And Colt Huddleston, the strongest person I know.

I could name another hundred people and give a thousand reasons why they deserve to be thanked by name, but then being mentioned in my first book wouldn't be as special. I want Carol and Colt to have bragging rights!

So, I'll just leave you (yes, you, the one person still reading) with a poem by John Quincy Adams. It's called Retrospection.

> When life's fair dream has passed away
> To three score years and ten,
> Before we turn again to clay
> The lot of mortal men,
> 'Tis wise a backward eye to cast
> On life's revolving scene,
> With calmness to review the past
> And ask what we have been.
> The cradle and the mother's breast
> Have vanish'd from the mind,
> Of joys the sweetest and the best,
> Nor left a trace behind.
> Maternal tenderness and care

Were lavished all in vain
Of bliss; whatever was our share
No vestiges remain.
Far distant, like a beacon light
On ocean's boundless waste,
A single spot appears in sight
Yet indistinctly traced.
Some mimic stage's thrilling, cry,
Some agony of fear,
Some painted wonder to the eye,
Some trumpet to the ear.
These are the first events of life
That fasten on the brain,
And through the world's incessant strife
Indelibly remain.
They form the link with ages past
From former worlds a gleam;
With murky vapors overcast,
The net-work of a dream.

Bibliography

Adams, John Quincy, and Worthington Chauncey Ford. *Writings of John Quincy Adams*. New York: Macmillan, 1913. Print.

Adams, John Quincy. *Diary of John Quincy Adams*. Cambridge, MA: Belknap of Harvard UP, 1981. Print.

---. *An Address Delivered at the Request of a Committee of the Citizens of Washington*. Washington: Davis and Force, 1821. Print.

Braude, Jacob Morton. *Speaker's Desk Book of Quips, Quotes, and Anecdotes*. Englewood Cliffs, NJ: Prentice-Hall, 1963. Print.

Burleigh, Anne Husted. *John Adams*. New Brunswick: Transaction, 2009. Print.

Butterfield, Lyman Henry *Adams Family Correspondence*. New York: Atheneum, 1965. Print.

---. *Diary and Autobiography of John Adams*. Cambridge, MA: Belknap of Harvard UP, 1961. Print.

Dickins, Asbury, and James C. Allen. *American State Papers: Documents, Legislative and Executive, of the Congress of the United States*. Washington: Gales and Seaton, 1858. Print.

Frank, Andrew. *American Revolution: People and Perspectives*. Santa Barbara, CA: ABC-CLIO, 2008. Print.

Kaplan, Fred. *John Quincy Adams: American Visionary*. New York, NY: HarperCollins, 2014. Print.

Koch, Adrienne, and William Peden. *The Selected Writings of John and John Quincy Adams*. New York: A.A. Knopf, 1946. Print.

Levin, Phyllis Lee. *Abigail Adams: A Biography*. New York: St. Martin's, 1987. Print.

---. *The Remarkable Education of John Quincy Adams*. New York: St. Martin's, 2015. Print.

Lincoln, Robert W. *Lives of the Presidents of the United States; with Biographical Notices of the Signers of the Declaration of Independence; Sketches of the Most Remarkable Events in the History of the Country*. Brattleboro', VT: Brattleboro' Typographic, 1839. Print.

Nagel, Paul C. *John Quincy Adams: A Public Life, a Private Life*. New York: Knopf, 1997. Print.

Remini, Robert V. *Henry Clay: Statesman for the Union*. New York: W.W. Norton, 1991. Print.

Renehan, Edward. *The Monroe Doctrine: The Cornerstone of American Foreign Policy*. New York: Chelsea House, 2007. Print.

Traub, James. *John Quincy Adams: Militant Spirit*. New York: Basic, 2016. Print.

Unger, Harlow G. John Quincy Adams. Boston: Da Capo, 2012. Print.

Timeline

1767 On July 11, John Adams' wife Abigail gave birth to her second child and first son. She named him John Quincy Adams.

1768 John Adams moved his family from Braintree to Boston, the city at the heart of the American Revolution.

1775 The Revolutionary War began.

1776 On July 4, The Declaration of Independence was signed by 56 delegates, including John Adams.

1778 John Quincy Adams left the USA with his father. They went to France on a ship named *Boston*, hoping to get their country the help it needed in the war.

1779 John Quincy left Paris to go to Russia with Francis Dana, an American minister. Francis Dana did not speak Russian or French (which was spoken by many educated Russians) and needed the boy to translate for him.

1783 The 16-year-old left Russia to join his father who was living in Holland. The two returned to France later that year. Meanwhile, the Revolutionary War was won by the United States.

1785 John Quincy Adams went back to the U.S. and like his father and grandfather before him, he attended Harvard.

1787 An ace student, he graduated second in his class with a Bachelor of Arts degree.

1789 George Washington, having easily won election, was sworn in as the first U.S. President. John Adams was sworn in as the first Vice President.

1790 John Quincy Adams passed his Massachusetts bar exam and became an attorney in Boston.

1794 President George Washington, having read several political articles by John Quincy Adams, was so impressed that he made him the USA's first minister to Holland.

1795 John Quincy Adams met his future wife, Louisa Catherine Johnson, in England.

1796 John Adams and Thomas Jefferson ran against each other in the first ever competitive presidential election. John Adams won.

1797 John Adams appointed John Quincy Adams minister of Prussia. John Quincy Adams married Louisa Johnson on July 26.

1800 John Adams and Thomas Jefferson battled for the presidency again. This time, Jefferson won, becoming the third U.S. President.

1802 John Quincy was elected to the Massachusetts Senate.

1803 John Quincy was appointed by members of the Massachusetts Senate to represent his state in the U.S. Senate.

1808 James Madison won the presidency.

1809 John Quincy was appointed minister to Russia by Madison.

1812 The United States declared war on Britain.

1813 Madison called on John Quincy to negotiate peace with the British.

1814 After a long negotiation, the Treaty of Ghent is signed by British and American officials, including John Quincy.

1815 John Quincy took office as minister to Britain.

1816   James Monroe won the presidency.

1817   John Quincy was appointed to serve as secretary of state by James Monroe.

1818   Abigail Adams passed away.

1819   John Quincy negotiated the purchase the purchase of Florida from Spain.

1823   John Quincy wrote the Monroe Doctrine.

1824   The 1824 Presidential Election ended without any candidate receiving a majority of the electoral vote, resulting in the House of Representatives having to decide the winner.

1825   John Quincy was appointed by the House of Representatives to serve as president.

1826   John Adams passed away.

1828   Andrew Jackson defeated John Quincy in the 1828 Presidential Election.

1829   John Quincy's oldest son, George Washington Adams, passed away.

1830 John Quincy was elected to the U.S. House of Representatives.

1834 His second oldest son, John Adams II, passed away.

1844 John Quincy defeated the Gag Rule that had banned Congressional debate of slavery. It was a huge victory for freedom of speech and a huge blow to the pro-slavery movement.

1848 On February 23, John Quincy Adams passed away at age 80.

Glossary

Aqueducts Structures used to divert the flow of water.

Ample More than enough.

Bargain A deal or agreement.

Bated Nervously or in suspense.

Bellows An object that produces air when its two handles are pushed inward.

Canal A manmade waterway.

Coeval Of the same age.

Colleague A co-worker or teammate.

Compliance Obeying or cooperating with a command.

Constitutional In agreement with the laws put forth in the U.S. Constitution.

Contagious Able to spread easily.

Conviction Passion or energy.

Discredit To destroy the reputation of a person or group.

Deliberation Considering the facts at hand before making a decision.

Electioneering Trying to influence the outcome of an election.

Eulogy A statement, either spoken or in writing, honoring a deceased person.

Facilitate To bring about or make possible.

Faculty The teachers and administrators of a school.

Indiscretion A careless mistake.

Indolent Extremely lazy.

Inquiry A formal or official search for information.

Intellectual A person of great intelligence.

Legislation A law or set of laws.

Mesmerize To hypnotize someone or hold their attention.

Minimalistic As simple as possible.

Mudslinging Attacking the reputation of a person or group by using insults.

Negotiate To attempt to resolve an issue and or reach an agreement through debate.

Neutral Not favoring either side in an argument or conflict.

Nominate To name a person to receive something such as an award or office.

Obligations Duties expected of someone.

Pantaloons A type of old-fashioned baggy pants worn by women.

Predecessor The person who held an office before the one who currently holds it.

Repealed Reversed or canceled.

Rhetoric The art of speaking well or general use of language.

Sabotage The act of destroying something through trickery.

Sanctioned Officially approved of.

Scruple A moral doubt.

Slavocracy A government ruled by slave owners.

Solemnity The state or quality of being serious and dignified.

Speculative Not carefully grounded in fact; imaginative in nature.

Symbolic Representing something.

Tariff A tax on imported or exported goods.

Treason The act of betraying one's own country.

Index

About the Author

Edward Cody Huddleston is an author, editor, and poet who lives in Baxley, Georgia. He loves haiku and his own have appeared in over a dozen publications, including *Modern Haiku, The Heron's Nest, Presence* and *Shamrock*. He's the first haiku poet to have been featured in Tupelo Press's 30/30 Project.

He dedicates this book to the memories of Raymond Huddleston, Joseph Herbert, and Beverly Huddleston.

MIKE PURDY'S

PRESIDENTIALHISTORY.COM

Presidential History
NEWS

Original video web series featuring Mike Purdy delivering "live" TV news coverage of key moments in presidential history.

- Presidential Sites
- Books
- Speeches
- Other Blogs
- In the News
- Other Resources

Presidential History
RESOURCES

Presidential Historian Mike Purdy is regularly interviewed and quoted in the media including The Wall Street Journal, CNN, USA Today, Reuters, New York Daily News, and WHDT World News. Visit www.PresidentialHistory. com/about for a list with links of his media interviews.

Contact Mike Purdy

mike@PresidentialHistory.com
(206) 295-1464

Follow on Social Media

Mike Purdy
Presidential Historian

Twitter: twitter.com/PresHistory
Facebook: www.facebook.com/mikepurdypresidentialhistory
YouTube: www.youtube.com/user/preshistory
Pinterest: www.pinterest.com/PresHistory

MIKE PURDY'S
PRESIDENTIALHISTORY.com